THE SAN CARLOS INDIAN CATTLE INDUSTRY

HARRY T. GETTY

NUMBER 7

ANTHROPOLOGICAL PAPERS
OF THE UNIVERSITY OF ARIZONA

THE UNIVERSITY OF ARIZONA PRESS

TUCSON 1963

L.C. Card Catalog No. 63-11974

PREFACE

In the spring of 1953 the San Carlos Tribal Council and the superintendent of the San Carlos Apache Reservation approved a study of the origin, development, and present status of the cattle industry on that reservation. During the summers of 1953, 1954, and 1955 I carried on research on this problem.

The decision to study the cattle industry of the San Carlos Indians rested upon two points of interest. In the first place, several articles, essentially of a popular nature, had been written describing the cattle-raising activities of the San Carlos Indians. These articles had presented the matter in such a way that there seemed to have been no problems connected with the steady development of this industry. Also, it was made to appear that the San Carlos cattle industry had had no problems in 1953 or in the years immediately preceding. It seemed likely to me that any cooperative human activity such as this would have had operational problems.

The second point of interest was derived from the body of theory that has been developed regarding patterns of human life and the changes that occur in those patterns. To what extent could the changes in the San Carlos Indian cattle industry be related to current theories regarding culture change?

The research at San Carlos consisted primarily of studying the agency files regarding the cattle industry on the reservation. Some of the files contained only data on the cattle operations. Other files were only partially concerned with cattle raising, such as the minutes of the Tribal Council meetings, ordinances, and resolutions, and the annual reports of the superintendents of the San Carlos Agency. From these files, data pertinent to the cattle industry were recorded and analyzed in terms of historical development and theory of cultural anthropology.

Analysis of the recorded data raised questions regarding the origin and development of the cattle industry on the reservation. These questions were discussed with many people, both on and off the reservation, who were then or had been connected with the reservation cattle operations. Indians of various ages were consulted. Current or past members of the local staff of the Bureau of Indian Affairs provided additional data bearing on the questions.

It is impossible to name here all the Indians on the San Carlos Reservation who aided in this study. Clarence Wesley, Jess Stevens, George Stevens, Britton Goode, and Fred Naltazan all gave strong support. But there were many others who contributed in the course of formal and informal interviews.

Thomas H. Dodge was the superintendent who approved this research project and then provided continuing encouragement. His successor, Charles J. Rives, has made assistance available in a variety of forms. Other members of the agency staff who have rendered invaluable aid are Paul Buss, Minor E. (Bill) Linn, Mrs. Ethel Jennings, Albert R. Purchase, and Alden W. Jones.

Escom Wheeler, who was employed by the Tribal Council as the general manager of tribal enterprises for a number of years, and his predecessor, Thomas R. Shiya, both contributed highly useful information and advice. Another tribal employee who was very helpful was Gunter Prude, the present manager, Tribal Livestock Operations.

My special thanks are due the American Philosophical Society, Philadelphia, which provided the financial support for the field work carried on in the summers of 1954 and 1955.

Several people, both Indian and non-Indian, read the manuscript and offered criticisms and suggestions, for which I am very grateful. The staff of the Department of Anthropology, University of Arizona, gave freely of assistance and advice.

Deep appreciation is due my wife, who offered constant encouragement and who assisted in numerous ways, especially in doing most of the final typing.

All photographs in this study are through the courtesy of the Branch of Land Operations, Bureau of Indian Affairs, United States Department of the Interior.

Harry T. Getty

University of Arizona
December, 1962

The tribal store and office at San Carlos.

CONTENTS

Eradicating juniper with a bulldozer on the Point of Pines range. Juniper crowds out the forage grasses.

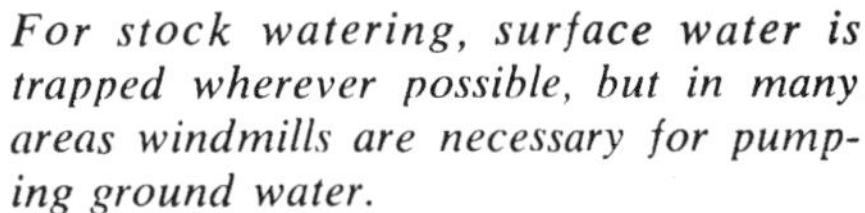

For stock watering, surface water is trapped wherever possible, but in many areas windmills are necessary for pumping ground water.

Preparing chow for a roundup crew.

Part of the tribal registered herd.

A roundup camp on the Ash Creek range.

A cattle sale at the Calva pens.

1 INTRODUCTION

As Indian reservations were established in the western United States in the decades following the Civil War, the government of the United States began definite efforts to change the lifeways of these Indians. These efforts were aimed at eliminating Indian customs and replacing them with the customs and practices which were current among the English-speaking people who were populating the West in the 1870's, and also at getting the Indian people on a self-sustaining basis on their reservations areas.

In the case of the Indians on the San Carlos Reservation little progress in this latter direction was made for many years. This reservation was established in 1872 and certain groups of Indians, principally Apaches, were placed within its boundaries. Fifty years, however, elapsed before organized efforts were made to get these Indians into the cattle-raising business as a method of achieving economic self-sufficiency.

This sort of programmed change has been referred to by Ralph Linton as directed culture change (1940:502):

> Directed culture change will be taken to refer to those situations in which one of the groups in contact interferes actively and purposefully with the culture of the other. This interference may take the form of stimulating the acceptance of new culture elements, inhibiting the exercise of preexisting culture patterns, or, as seems to be most frequently the case, doing both simultaneously.

If one of the groups in contact is able to interfere actively and purposefully with the culture of the other, then the first group is in a dominant position, and the second group is in a subordinate position. This is one of the necessary conditions for directed culture change (Linton 1940:502-03; Spicer 1961:7-8). Linton (1940:502) indicates that the group which is interfering with the culture of another group is doing so in order to change the culture of the latter group so as to make it conform as much as possible to the culture of the interfering group. Spicer (1961:7-8) considers this to be the second condition necessary to define a contact situation as one of directed culture change.

It is considered here that the development of the cattle industry of the San Carlos Indians is a case of directed culture change. On the basis of this consideration, the development of that Indian cattle industry should be analyzed in terms of several concepts that have been developed in regard to culture change.

Linton (1936:403-11) proposes that the concepts of form, meaning, use, and function be utilized in the analysis of culture, and particularly in situations of culture change. In this analysis of the San Carlos Indian cattle industry, the concept of use is omitted. Linton says in regard to this concept, "It seems safe to say that all trait complexes possess at least meaning and function, although use cannot always be ascribed to them under our definition" (1936:405). He points out that the form of a culture element, complex, or activity may be transferred, but in the process may assume different meanings and functions. Has this proved to be the case with the San Carlos cattle industry?

It will also be well to consider the idea proposed by Linton that new culture elements, complexes, or activities may (1) remain as cultural alternatives; (2) become specialties in the culture; or (3) be generally accepted and become universals in the culture. On this basis, the question can be asked: Did cattle raising become a universal with the San Carlos Indians?

It would appear that directed culture change may involve all, or most, aspects of a subordinate culture, or the selection of certain aspects. In the case of the San Carlos Reservation, and on numerous other reservations, practically all aspects of culture have been subjected to directed culture change. Some aspects, particularly those concerned with subsistence, were more susceptible to change than others.

It would be wise at this point to outline the distribution of the Indian people on the San Carlos Reservation. From the earliest days of the reservation the Indian population has been concentrated in a few communities. For most of the years following the establishment of the reservation the Indians were concentrated in three communities – Bylas, Old San Carlos, and Rice. With the building of Coolidge Dam in 1929 and the development of the reservoir behind the dam, Old San Carlos was covered by the impounded water. The Bureau of Indian Affairs Agency was moved from Old San Carlos to Rice, and the name of the latter was changed to San Carlos – the present community of that name.

At the new community of San Carlos the agency buildings were developed in an area immediately northwest of the junction of Gilson Creek with the San Carlos River. In recent years this area has been surrounded by a barbed-wire fence, with a road entrance on the south side. Inside this rather sizeable barbed-wire enclosure were located the agency office building, one part of which was used for tribal offices; residences for most of the agency personnel; the hospital; the school; the Employees' Club; the garage; and other agency buildings. In December 1949 the Tribal Council purchased a general store which was operating at San Carlos. This, also, was located inside the fenced enclosure. In January 1952 the council also bought a general store at Bylas on U.S. Highway 80 in the southeastern part of the reservation. Both stores are still operated by the Tribal Council.

On the south side of the agency area is Gilson Creek. Across this are the railroad, post office, privately owned trading posts, and some Apache residences. To the east, and extending for some distance north of the agency area, are Apache residences. Apaches are also located west of the agency along Gilson Creek, and south along the San Carlos River to Peridot.

Thus, so far as the main community of San Carlos is concerned, the agency area is centrally located, and is, therefore, in a position to exert maximum influence in directing culture change.

Since the agency and tribal offices are located at San Carlos, the people of Bylas have been forced to look to San Carlos for all sorts of decisions.

Throughout most of the year a few Apaches are located on the various ranges. Otherwise, the Indian population is concentrated in the communities of San Carlos and Bylas. The result of this geographical relationship between the Indian communities, the agency, and the ranges has been the keeping of the Indians in close touch with the agency personnel, but with no sustained contact with their cattle on the ranges. The Indians have been content to let agency personnel handle the matters pertaining to the cattle industry, or to operate under instructions from the agency people.

With the advantageous position enjoyed by the Bureau of Indian Affairs, it could be expected that the personnel of that organization would exploit their advantage in directing culture change on the San Carlos Reservation. The facts are that through the years the Bureau of Indian Affairs personnel on the San Carlos Reservation were quite willing to make full use of their position of advantage as representatives of the dominant society in the United States. Since the establishment of the reservation, the Indians had become accustomed to the bureau assuming responsibility for their welfare, and most of them were content with the continuation of this system. The demonstration of this fact is one of the purposes of this volume.

Erasmus (1954:147-58) points out several factors which should be considered in analyzing a case of directed culture change and which he believes are generally present in such situations—empiricism, need, cooperation, inducement, and complexity. With regard to empiricism he says:

> Introduced changes that bear clear and immediate proof of their effectiveness and desirability usually achieve a more rapid and wide-

> spread acceptance than changes of long-term benefit or changes in which the relationship between the new technic and its purported results is not easily grasped on the basis of casual observation.

Fisher (1953:142), reporting on a study of directed culture change in Nayarit, Mexico, makes a similar observation: "Overt customs with obvious reward advantage will have more stimulus value than abstract items, mental patterns, customs with delayed or indirect reward, and so on."

One of the most important, if not the most important, of the factors outlined by Erasmus is need.

> The needs felt by the people, as distinguished from those felt by the innovators, constitute one of the most important factors pertaining to the acceptability of an innovation, in any particular case. If the people fail to feel or to recognize the need for an innovation, it may prove impossible to introduce it on a voluntary basis.

Referring to a specific case involving ailments afflicting a group, Erasmus comments that

> thus, despite the fact that they feel a general need for assistance in combatting the ailments common among them, they may fail to perceive the need for the specific measures proposed and may actively resist them.

This would seem to indicate a failure in communications between those people directing the culture change and those being affected by the change. Spicer (1952:18) verifies this opinion when he says:

> We begin to see resistance as a symptom of something wrong in the cross-cultural situation, perhaps of the real impracticality of the proposed change, perhaps of unsatisfactory relations between the worker and the people.

Coupled with the matter of needs being realized by the subordinate group is the very important process of planning *with* the group, not *for* it, the means of satisfying the felt needs. It is this writer's conviction that any program of directed culture change – not enforced change – stands a good chance of failing unless those who are to benefit by the change are full partners in the planning activities.

Erasmus recognizes that culture change is discussed in terms of individuals, but he also points out that

> some changes may require group or community adoption, a circumstance that can greatly increase the operational difficulties of introducing them.

So far as the factor of inducement is concerned, if the planning is carefully and cooperatively done then there should be no need for inducement, or at least a minimum amount of that kind of effort should be required.

Complexity is a characteristic of any culture. This becomes more evident when an effort is made to alter any part of the culture pattern. As Erasmus states,

> Frequently a change which seems desirable to the innovator may depend upon so many other secondary accompanying changes that its introduction is difficult.

To what extent were these five factors operative in the development of the San Carlos cattle industry? To what extent should they be expected to operate in culture-change situations similar to that under discussion here?

In view of the relationship, geographical and otherwise, between the Bureau of Indian Affairs personnel and the Indians on the San Carlos Reservation it might by hypothesized here that the five factors of directed culture change stated by Erasmus would be found to have operated in the following manner:

1. The factor of empiricism would not have been thought of by bureau personnel. In fact, it probably would have been difficult to achieve short-term results in the development of the Indian cattle industry.
2. It could be expected that the bureau personnel would recognize the needs of the Indians in regard to the long-term development of the Indian cattle industry, but that the Indians, in general, would not be aware of such needs. Failure on the part of the Indians to realize these needs would likely result in an attitude of apathy toward the cattle industry.
3. The combination of a feeling of responsibility on the part of the bureau personnel and the attitude of apathy on the part of the Indians toward the cattle industry could be expected to result in a lack of cooperative effort in this subsistence activity. It could be expected that

too much would be done *for* the Indians and not enough *with* them. In many respects this would be an easier way out for both parties.

4. Given the attitudes of responsibility on the one hand, and apathy on the other, it would be expected that there would be little effort at inducement made by the representatives of the dominant group. Any such efforts that might be made would likely be insufficient, and faced by a wall of apathy.
5. Since all aspects of a culture are interrelated, it could be expected that change in any one aspect would affect, and be affected by, the other aspects. It would be expected, therefore, that the development of the cattle industry would affect other aspects of Apache culture, but that it would, in turn, be affected by the values prevalent in other aspects of Apache culture. These Apache cultural values might be expected to retard the development of a successful cattle industry, as seen from a non-Indian point of view.

In view of the operations of the federal government on this and other reservation areas, it could be further hypothesized that cattle raising in a government-managed community could be expected to be another "government activity," functioning to reinforce feelings of dependency on the federal government on the part of the Indians.

By way of contrast, it could be pointed out that in non-reservation situations cattle raising is a specialty. It is a source of individual stimulus and development through private enterprise.

The question here is whether or not in a government-managed community cattle raising could ever be a stimulus to private enterprise.

In his study of Navaho veterans, Vogt (1951: 88-89) recognized "four 'stages' in the transition from Navaho to white American ways of life."

> 1) In the first "stage" there is minimal contact with whites, and the individual Navaho manifests the characteristics of the Navaho value system – as it was transmitted to him in his family and "outfit."
>
> 2) Increased effective contacts with the dominant white culture bring about an imitative "stage" in which selected value patterns of the dominant culture are *imitated* but not internalized. . . . In short, the new patterns are merely externals.
>
> 3) At a much later period and after years of sustained white contact, a more fundamental shift occurs in which white value patterns begin to be *internalized*. These individuals no longer merely verbalize certain white values that are enshrined in the dominant culture, but these values come to be integral parts of their motivational systems.
>
> 4) In a final possible "stage" the acculturation reaches the point where the residuals of Navaho value-orientations are lost and the individual Navaho is culturally indistinguishable from whites of the same age and sex.

Vogt felt that in the series of case histories he presented most of the individuals seemed to be "at various points in the second or imitative 'stage' of acculturation." The question at this point is, where do the San Carlos Indians stand in regard to these stages of transition?

The terms "innovation" and "innovator" have been and will be used in this report. As defined by Barnett (1953:7), "An innovation is . . . any thought, behavior, or thing that is new because it is qualitatively different from existing forms." Although this writer has not found a clear-cut definition of an innovator, not even by Barnett, it would seem that the innovator is the individual who devises or introduces any qualitatively new thought, behavior, or thing.

These are some of the concepts and principles which should prove useful in analyzing the development of the cattle industry of the San Carlos Indians. Whether or not they are useful tools for this purpose will be seen in the following pages.

This monograph is not intended to be a criticism of the Bureau of Indian Affairs in developing the San Carlos cattle operations. In the opinion of this writer such criticism would serve no purpose at this point in time. Rather, it is an effort to see what factors that were operative in this situation have been present in other instances of culture change and might be found in similar situations of directed culture change at the present time or in the future.

2 HISTORICAL SKETCH – WESTERN APACHES

Aboriginal Subsistence Activities

In order to have a sound understanding of the way in which the Indians on the San Carlos Reservation have reacted to the efforts made to develop a cattle industry among them, it is necessary to outline the probable nature of their aboriginal subsistence activities. Information of this type is largely inferential. Such data as are available have been recorded by Spanish, Mexican, and nineteenth-century American observers. Goodwin, in his volume, *The Social Organization of the Western Apache,* has combined documentary data with statements made by Indian informants, to provide a reconstruction of the aboriginal culture of the Western Apache. The following statements regarding aboriginal Apache subsistence are based on Goodwin's volume, and refer only to the San Carlos Group.

Relative to the present concentration of the Indian people in two major communities on the San Carlos Reservation, it is important to note the following statement made by Goodwin (1942: 160):

> Despite the seasonal residences in other places, the real ties were with the home locality about the farming site. Although some wild-food crops were occasionally stored in caves close to where they were gathered, the greatest portions were packed home, often over miles of rugged country, to be stored in ground cache, cave, tree cache, or wickiup, where they would be available throughout the winter. The most permanent and largest wickiups were always contructed here....

Goodwin outlines the annual cycle of subsistence activities and the associated group movements. In April parties of people moved into the mountain ranges on either side of the Gila River from Black River to the Santa Catalina Mountains to collect and process mescal. The prepared mescal was then taken back to the permanent camp. In May the various farming areas were planted, and the irrigation ditches were cleaned and repaired. "Farm-owning families usually stayed until the corn was up six or eight inches in the first part of July. After that, only a few old people, sometimes captives, were left in charge of the farms, the rest moving away" (Goodwin 1942:156). During the early part of July, groups of people gathered the fruit of the saguaro cactus in the valleys of the Gila and San Pedro rivers. The most important wild food, the acorn of the Emory oak, was harvested in late July. Practically everyone participated in this harvest. The highlands on either side of the Gila River, the foothills on the southwest side of the Pinaleño range, and the area around the present community of Oracle on the north side of the Catalina Mountains, supported some of the best of the oak groves. These gathering activities were usually carried on by extended-family groups. They might stay at the oak groves for a month or more. Mesquite beans were ripe along the Gila, San Carlos, and San Pedro rivers in late August, but this was not an important food item for the Apaches. During September and October the people were busy at the farms, harvesting and storing the crops. Piñon nuts and juniper berries were ripe in November. They were abundant in the high country to the north of the Gila river and on the slopes of the Pinaleño Mountains south of the river.

Goodwin points out that "thus, from April until November, the Apache's time was divided between farming, gathering wild foods, and hunting, covering in all a very wide territory" (1942: 158). Furthermore, he stresses the importance of the extended family as the functional unit in all these gathering activities.

From the end of November to the first of April hunting was practically the only subsistence activity. Parties of men hunted deer throughout the various mountain ranges. This was also a time for visiting and for raiding. Many of the Apaches residing in the White Mountains moved south to the Gila valley and to the slopes on either side of the valley to escape the bitter winter weather of the higher country.

For some period of time prior to the establishment of the reservations, raiding seems to have been an activity characteristic of all Western Apache groups. At least one of the functions of these raids was the augmenting of the natural resources available to any unit of Apaches. According to Goodwin, the groups of the Western Apaches did not raid each other. Relations with neighboring Indians varied from time to time. With the Navajo, relations were "intermittently friendly and hostile, always distrustful. Navaho raided and made war against the White Mountain, Cibecue, Southern Tonto and Northern Tonto peoples, who in similar manner attacked the Navaho" (1942:72). In regard to the Hopi, "relations on the whole seem to have been friendly, though infrequent Apache raids occurred" (1942:74). The same thing seems to have been true in regard to the Zuni. Definite hostility characterized the relations between the Western Apaches and the Papagos and Pimas. Those Western Apache groups adjacent to the Papagos and Pimas raided these groups continually, particularly during the winter months. The Papagos and Pimas made retaliatory raids, particularly on the San Carlos and Southern Tonto groups.

Spanish Period

Chronicles of the early Spanish expeditions into the area now included in the states of Arizona and New Mexico do not indicate any definite contact with, or knowledge of, the Western Apaches. These include the expeditions of Coronado in 1540–42, Espejo in 1582–83, and Oñate in 1598. However, Goodwin (1942:66) points out that "this should not be taken as conclusive evidence that none lived there. Apache camps were well hidden, and Apache did not show themselves to forces as imposing as Coronado's." The Benavides Memorial of 1634 (Hodge *et al* 1945:81) speaks of Apaches occupying the whole of New Mexico.

The *Rudo Ensayo* (p. 139) states that in 1686 the Apaches were raiding the Opatas, a tribe located in the central part of what is now the Mexican state of Sonora. There is no identification of the Apache raiders as to group or band. However, many of the Spanish documents of this time and of the eighteenth century state that the Apache raiding parties came from "Chiquicaqui" (Chiricahua) Mountains. Spanish punitive expeditions from Sonora often went as far as this mountain range in what is now the southeastern corner of the state of Arizona. Since it was, undoubtedly, the Chiricahua Apaches who were making these raids into Sonora, it is not clear whether or not Indians of the San Carlos group were making similar raids at this time. They definitely did so at a later date.

Most of the Spanish maps of the seventeenth and eighteenth centuries show a blank space in what is now eastern and southeastern Arizona, and show therein the single term "Apachería." This void is verified by Bolton (1936:23) in writing of the Jesuits in New Spain. Referring to the northward movement of the Jesuits through Sonora, he says that "now, on the northeast, they were blocked by Apaches, as by a Chinese wall."

Bolton (1936:244–45) gives a very clear statement of the nature of the relationships between the Apaches and the Spanish.

> When first heard of, the Apaches, though warlike, covered a narrow range and were devoted somewhat to agriculture. But the Spaniards brought horses to the frontier, the Apaches acquired them, and their range widened. The Spaniards had also vast herds of cattle which the Apaches came to prize as food. In other words, the Spaniards raised stock and at the same time gave the Apaches the means of stealing it. As the 17th century waned, the raids became longer and longer, until by Kino's day the Apaches not only ravaged border missions and outlying ranches, but penetrated the very heart of Sonora, supplementing theft with fire and murder. The blame was not one-sided. Spanish soldiery pursued the invaders, slew the warriors when they could catch them, captured women and children and kept them as slaves. The Spanish-American soldiery were as ruthless as the Anglo-Americans who a century and a half later

> inherited the hatred of the children of these same sons of the desert.
>
> The Apache has left his mark on the map. His resistance stopped the Spanish advance about where the line was finally fixed between two nations.

Goodwin points out that in addition to Chiricahua Apaches, raids were made on central Sonora by the White Mountain Apaches. The Cibecue and San Carlos groups raided some of the settlements in northern Sonora, but concentrated on the Pimas and Papagos. Regarding the situation in Sonora, Goodwin states (1942:93–94):

> The size of the territory in Sonora over which the Western Apache raided is extraordinary. The Apache knew it like their own country, and every mountain, town, or spring of consequence had its Apache name. . . . It was not unusual for a party to be gone seventy or eighty days. Raids brought the Apache horses, mules, burros, cattle, cloth, clothing, blankets, metal to be made into spearheads, arrowpoints or knives, occasionally firearms, saddles, bridles, leather, cowhide for moccasin soles, and anything else light and useful which could be brought home. Animals obtained were commonly killed and eaten, as the Western Apache made little effort at raising stock in prereservation times.

It is this last point that is the important one for this study of the Apache cattle industry. Many writers—Spanish, Mexican, and American—point out that one of the main purposes of the Apache raids was the driving off of livestock. However, few of the writers indicate how the Apaches used the livestock. With a group as mobile as the Apaches apparently were, it is unlikely that they would have possessed either the opportunity or the inclination to make any deliberate effort to raise livestock. When supplies ran low, it was usually possible to make another raid. Of course, some of the horses were kept for transportation.

Another purpose of the raids into Sonora was to secure livestock to trade to Spanish-speaking people in New Mexico. The *Rudo Ensayo* states: "At least it cannot be doubted that the same Indians who ravage Sonora go every year to the fair of New Mexico, as is shown by the brands on Sonora's cattle carried to that market" (1951: 88). It is probable that the term "cattle" is used here in a rather general sense, including horses. Goodwin (1942:94) states that "they [Apaches] traded with certain New Mexicans who ventured into the Western Apache country to obtain the same horses and mules taken in turn from Mexicans to the south."

Mexican Period

After the people of Mexico gained their independence in 1823 they were in no better position to control raiding on the northern frontier than the Spanish government had been. The Apaches, realizing the change that was in process, took full advantage of the situation, pushing their raids ever deeper into Sonora, and making them more frequently. Sonora became, in fact, a supply depot for the Apaches. Raids continued unabated throughout the period of Mexican control of Arizona and New Mexico.

American Period — Pre-Reservation

Quite some time before the United States took over control of the area that is now Arizona and New Mexico, English-speaking men had made their way through this region. In 1807 Zebulon M. Pike was in the area of New Mexico where he had an opportunity to observe Apaches. Early in 1825 a group of American trappers under the leadership of a man by the name of James O. Pattie encountered a band of Apaches in the Gila valley in eastern Arizona, near the location of the present-day community of Fort Thomas. The trappers were attacked by the Apaches, who later protested that they thought the trappers were Spanish. In 1828 another group of trappers fought a short battle with Apaches in the White Mountain region.

With the outbreak of the war with Mexico in 1846, General Kearny proclaimed in Las Vegas, New Mexico, that the government of the United States was taking control of New Mexico, and that the peaceful people were thereby guaranteed protection against raiding Indians. Furthermore, in the Treaty of Guadalupe Hidalgo which concluded the war with Mexico in 1848, the government of the United States agreed to prevent Indians residing in the new portions of the United States from raiding into Mexico. It was one thing to make these promises, but it was quite another thing to keep them. For a period of 40 years hostile relationships continued between the United States and the Apaches, with the latter raiding both Americans and Mexicans.

These Apache raids continued to have as one of their main motives the securing of supplies, particularly food. As before, one of the main operations in connection with any raid was the driving off of any livestock that was handy, particularly horses and cattle. One part of a raiding party would delay pursuit forces with rearguard action while the rest of the party drove the livestock on to a safe location. When a position of relative safety was achieved, some of the animals were butchered to provide an immediate meat supply. The remaining animals were usually driven back to the permanent camp, where most of them met a similar fate.

Reservation Period

Establishing the Reservation

> An executive order of November 9, 1871, established at Camp Apache, Arizona, the White Mountain Reservation, formerly set aside by the War Department as an Indian reservation for Apaches. Executive order of December 14, 1872, added the San Carlos Division. . . . An act of June 7, 1897, provided that the portion of the White Mountain or San Carlos Reservation north of the Salt or Black River should be known as the Fort Apache Reservation (Kelly 1953: 23).

In his 1935 annual report the superintendent of the San Carlos Reservation gave an additional bit of history of the reservation, which he referred to as a jurisdiction.

> The San Carlos jurisdiction was originally divided into three districts, the Bylas or southern district, the San Carlos or headquarters district, and the Rice or northern district. On account of the construction of the Coolidge dam, the entire agency and agricultural area of the San Carlos district was destroyed and covered by the San Carlos Lake. At the present time, we have the two remaining districts, Bylas and what was formerly Rice, but which was later and at present called the San Carlos District, which now includes the agency administration.

In the years 1873, 1874, 1877, 1893, 1896, and 1902 large areas of land were removed from the eastern, southern, and western sides of the original reservation and were restored to public domain. The total acreage removed was 2,814,136, leaving the present reservation of 1,643,939 acres.

Concentration of Indians on the Reservation

After the establishment of the San Carlos Reservation, the federal government adopted a policy which called for the concentration on that reservation of various Apache groups and bands, as well as the Yavapais. Statements regarding this concentration indicate that economy of administration was one motive. Another motive, closely allied to that of economy, was the feeling that it would be easier to control the hostile Indians if they were concentrated on one reservation.

Goodwin (1942:15) states that "in 1875 all the Apache bands were moved to the Gila River, owing to government policy of concentration."

John G. Bourke, an army officer who participated in numerous campaigns against the Apaches (1891:660), took a very dim view of the policy of concentration.

> There is no brighter page in our Indian history than that which records the progress of the subjugated Apaches at Camp Apache and Camp Verde, nor is there a fouler blot than that which conceals the knavery which secured their removal to the junction of the San Carlos and Gila.

When John P. Clum became Indian agent at San Carlos on August 8, 1874, the Apaches on the reservation seem to have been members of the Pinal, Aravaipa, and Tonto bands (Goodwin, 1942:209). Most of them had been moved from Camp Grant in 1873.

In April of 1873 Yavapais (known as Mohave-Apaches and Yuma-Apaches) and Tonto Apaches surrendered to General Crook and were established on a reservation at Camp Verde. However, early in 1875 the government ordered that they be moved to San Carlos. Enroute to San Carlos serious fighting broke out between groups of the Indians being moved, and the troops escorting them had considerable difficulty in controlling the situation. Even at San Carlos matters were difficult because the Apaches already on the reservation were at enmity with many of the Indians who were being moved in. Regarding the Yavapai contingent, Goodwin (1942:91-92) says: "During the last decade of the nineteenth century and the first decade of the twentieth, almost all of them returned to their former habitat, though a few still remain on the San Carlos Reservation."

In 1875 the White Mountain Apaches were moved to San Carlos. By 1880 most of the Eastern band had returned to their old homes around Fort Apache. The small number that remained settled at Bylas in 1911 and 1912, where they are still living. In like manner, most of the Western band returned to the White Mountains in 1880; those remaining also settled eventually at Bylas.

Army officers in charge of field operations vigorously opposed the moving of the Indians from both Camp Verde and Camp Apache. Their well-founded objections were, however, overruled by government officials in Washington.

Along with the other Western Apaches the Cibecue group was removed to San Carlos in 1875, but after a few years the major portion of them returned to the Cibecue valley.

In May, 1876, Clum received telegraphic orders to proceed with his force of Apache police to Apache Pass – at the northern end of the Chiricahua Mountains – take over the Chiricahua Agency, and remove those Indians to San Carlos. This was accomplished by June 18th. This move seems to have been an unwise one, partly because the abolition of the Chiricahua Reservation broke faith with those Indians, and partly because it placed another Apache group on a reservation already plagued by intergroup antipathies. During the next ten years many of the Chiricahuas were off the San Carlos Reservation more than they were on it.

At the time of this study, 1953–55, the Indian groups recognized on the San Carlos Reservation were: San Carlos, White Mountain (Coyotero), Mohave (Yavapai), and Tonto. The extent to which these groups figure in tribal operations today, and especially in connection with the cattle industry, will become evident in subsequent parts of this report.

Included in the answers on a Bureau of Indian Affairs questionnaire in 1934 was the following statement by the superintendent at San Carlos regarding the membership of the local tribal business committee.

> Members of this Committee were selected by districts according to population. Bylas has two members, being the Coyoteros and Chiricahuas; San Carlos four, being what is known as the San Carlos or local band of Indians; Mohaves one, representing certain Mohave Indians moved from the Camp Verde and Ft. McDowell, Indians who moved to this jurisdiction many years ago and who have since made their homes here. The Mohave Indians live in and together with the San Carlos Apaches since the flooding of the Coolidge Dam area but at that time had a separate area of land.

The term Coyotero usually refers to the White Mountain Apaches, while Mohave is the short form of Mohave-Apache, which is one of the terms used to refer to the Yavapais.

Tag-Band Designations

It is impossible to understand human relationships on the Western Apache reservations during the first 50 years after they were established without some knowledge of the tag bands. These designations for groups were established by government personnel as a convenient means of systematizing daily contacts with the Apaches. It was difficult, if not impossible, for English-speaking people to use Apache names. Particularly during the period when rations were furnished the Apaches, frequent contact with families, or heads of families, was necessary. Goodwin (1942:189-91) makes a rather satisfactory presentation of the facts concerning the tag-band system.

> Government usurping of chiefs' power and function has also helped to liquidate the local group. The government took over supervision of certain irrigation systems, controlled the food supply by rationing, and handled serious social misdemeanors in the reservation courts which it dominated. It did not hesitate to contradict and alter a chief's course of action. It created tag-band chiefs, some of whom were true chiefs, others being merely wealthy men found to be amenable to the whites, and an alien patrilineal system of inheritance for tag-band chieftainships was imposed. In an attempt to recognize some of the already existing social units and to form a method of reservation identification, early governmental authorities on the San Carlos and Fort Apache reservations divided the total population into lettered tag-bands, those on the San Carlos Reservation being listed with double letters, such as "CF" or "SL," etc., and those

on the Fort Apache Reservation as A, B, C, etc.

All married men were assigned a number in the tag band with which they were affiliated, and wives took the same number as their husbands. On the death of a man, his number was held open for the next man needing one. Tag-band numbers were allotted mainly according to residence after marriage. Each tag-band had a chief selected and recognized by the government, who always was given the number 1. When a tag-band chief died, another man was appointed in his place and given his number. All men were supposed to wear a metal tag about their necks, on which was stamped their number. On the San Carlos Reservation these metal tags are said to have been differently shaped for each tag-band. Actually, tag-bands in the beginning were composed of from one to two or three prereservation local groups coming from the same locality, and in almost all cases the local groups combined in one tag band came from the same aboriginal band. The tag-band system is rapidly going out of use now, as members are no longer allotted.

. . . Until 1895 tag-band chiefs functioned in many respects as true chiefs. At one time they drew the beef ration for their tag-bands and distributed it. They guaranteed payment on supplies bought by their people in the traders' stores, and credit could be obtained by merely presenting the borrowed metal identification tag of a tag-band chief, against whose account the amount was charged.

. . . .

By 1895 the change had become so great and government domination so established, there was less and less room for chiefs. In one or two instances tag-band chiefs, too keen and assertive to be duped, were removed from the chieftainship by the agency. . . . The few tag-band chiefs remaining are old, and when they die they will not be replaced.

Referring to the fact that government employees and other whites on the reservation used the tag-band designations to indicate specific Apaches, Goodwin (1942:523, 525) goes on to state that

the Apache copied them in this, and for many years tag-band identifications were often used as names. However, this custom is gradually passing out of use, for more than twenty years ago the government allotted personal and family names, the use of which has become recognized by both whites and Apache.

In regard to the change from tag-band designations to name, the superintendent's annual report for 1913 states that a full-blood Apache who was a graduate of Carlisle Indian School had been employed "to take an accurate census of the San Carlos and Fort Apache Indians and to rename them consistently with respect to family relationships, in order to do away with the so-called 'tag-names,' the use of which is repugnant to all ideas of civilization. . . ."

Nevertheless, reservation censuses in the agency offices at San Carlos, including a 1952 census, still show the tag-band affiliation of individual Indians.

The following conversation regarding tag-band designations took place between an elderly Apache man and this author:

"Do you recall your tag-band number?"

"Oh yes, it was ——."

"You say *was*. Do you use it now?"

"No! Nobody use them anymore."

"Did they when you were a boy?"

"Oh yes. They used them then. Everybody use them just like a name."

"Was your father's tag-band number —— also?

"Yes."

"So you took your father's number?"

"Yes."

"Did you have any brothers?"

"Yes, I have one."

"Did he take the same number?"

"Yes, he use same number."

"What about women when they get married, do they take their husband's number?"

"Sometimes they take their husband's number. Sometimes they keep their own."

"By the time the cattle associations were formed were tag-band numbers being used?"

"Yes, some."

"Would an association be formed around one tag-band, or clan?"

"No, the associations were all mixed."

Another elderly Apache man said that girls used their father's tag-band number until married, then they used their husband's. The boys in a family took successive numbers beyond that of the father, but using the same letters.

Goodwin's statement brings out the fact that the tag bands, or at least their chiefs, became political instruments which were manipulated by the government. Nevertheless, the tag-band system was a rather convenient device for dealing with the problem of rations for the Indian population.

Rationing

In the first part of this chapter it was shown that in pre-reservation times the subsistence activities of the Western Apaches were based on the hunting of animals, and the gathering of plant products, strongly supplemented by farming. Beginning with the Spanish period, raiding became an increasingly important subsistence activity.

With the establishment of the White Mountain and San Carlos reservations, and the subsequent concentration of a large number of Apaches on the latter, problems arose in regard to the subsistence of these Indians. An important factor was the desire of the military forces to keep the Indians in just a few locations on the reservation, so as to control their movements and thus prevent raiding. Since this policy gave little or no opportunity for hunting and gathering, and only slightly more for farming, it was necessary to provide food, clothing, and other items for the Indian people. In addition, reports covering the 1870's and 1880's indicate that most of the Indians on the San Carlos Reservation showed very little inclination to support themselves. The white man's government had seen fit to round them up and concentrate them in strange country, and among hostile Indian groups, so the government could just arrange to support them.

The quotation from Goodwin given in the previous discussion of tag bands indicates that one of the important functions of the tag-band chiefs was to draw beef rations for the group. This applied to all types of ration goods.

The few items of literature that provide information regarding the distribution of ration goods present conflicting statements as to the techniques used, particularly in regard to the issuing of beef.

C. T. Connell (1921:6), who had been employed to make a census of the Indians on the San Carlos Reservation around 1880, gave the following description of the issuing of rations at San Carlos.

> Ration day is a gala one for the many tribes, who are denoted by their dress, cut of the hair, paint upon the face, style of clothing and actions, and there is a mingling of Tontos, Coyoteros, Pinals, and Apache-Yumans, all, however, of the same breed, but at one time deadly enemies, and in a sense are yet, certain restraint keeping them peaceful.
>
> Every Friday the butchering of cattle for the issue took place at the slaughtering pens, which was performed by the Indians themselves under the supervision of an American. The weekly count and issue of ration tickets took place on Thursday of each week, and every man, woman and child was entitled to one ticket whether an hour or a hundred years old. Friday was issue day, the commissary building was of adobe and had in its eastern wall a window through which the Apaches received the stores furnished them by the government. . . . The heads of families drawing rations for a family or band filed in the one end of the passage, one at a time . . . and passing out at the other end with their supplies.
>
> Each person was entitled to receive in proportion as follows:
>
> Five and one-half pounds of flour
> Four ounces of beans
> Eight pounds of sugar to 100 rations
> Four pounds of coffee to 100 rations
> One pound of salt to 100 rations
> Soap, one small cake

For some reason or other Connell did not include beef in his list of ration supplies. This item was definitely a part of the ration system, at San Carlos as well as on other reservations.

Brig. Gen. Thomas H. Slavens, in his book describing San Carlos in the 1880's, also discussed the issuance of rations, particularly the distribution of beef (Slavens, 194–:81).

> The issue of beef was first on the hoof, but the Indians in running down and killing the cattle created such a commotion, the butchering was so badly done and the whole process so barbarous, that this method of issue was stopped, and the cattle slaughtered by regular butchers and issued as dressed beef. . . . As the rations were usually consumed as soon as issued the Indians were for the most part without food and eager for another issue.

In his report of 1871, Mr. Vincent Colyer, Commissioner of Indian Affairs, recommended the establishment of the "White Mountain or San Carlos Reserve." For the Indian population of this reservation he suggested that "one pound of beef and one pound of corn per capita be issued with salt daily, and sugar and coffee occasionally."

Several of the annual reports made by the agent at San Carlos contain statements regarding the ration foods, especially the way in which some of the Indians handled the beef issue. The report dated August 1, 1878, states:

> They are very anxious to obtain stock-cattle, and are trying to do so by saving up their weekly ration of beef until they have sufficient to draw one or more cows. One Indian has already accumulated 43 head, and the total number owned by the Indians in June last was 521 stock-cattle and 760 sheep.

The annual report dated August 11, 1879, refers to a contract made on March 26, 1879, for supplies for the Indian Service, and indicates that beef and flour were furnished to San Carlos on the basis of this contract. The report dated August 15, 1880, also mentions the delivery of beef and flour on the contract of 1879. This same report states that other ration supplies were received but does not specify what they were. According to the report dated August 9, 1883, the Apaches were assured of regular weekly rations. On August 31, 1886, the agent stated that a saving had been effected on the beef ration for the year just ended, and with that money 1633 yearling heifers were purchased, 1045 of them being issued to Indians at San Carlos and 588 to Indians at Fort Apache. He also said that "twenty-nine hundred and seventy-two Indians here receive rations every week." In August, 1888, the agent reported: "Rations are now issued to 3,396 Indians and constitute one-third of their livelihood."

Regarding the ration system at San Carlos, one elderly Apache man told this author:

> "The military counted Apaches each week near Six-Mile Bridge and issued tickets for rations, which were issued each Friday. But Indians were not used to the foods issued—flour and sugar especially. Ten pounds of beef were issued to each Indian. Some Indians didn't take the weekly ten pounds of beef, but waited until they could draw live cattle. Or heads of groups of families – called chiefs, but they weren't chiefs, they were just figureheads – could draw live cattle. Sometimes they butchered them, sometimes they saved them and began herds. Government also issued sheep, but they didn't do so well in the low country."

This statement bears out the indication in the annual report of 1878 that some of the Indians saved their weekly rations of beef until they could draw live cattle. This enabled many of them to get a start on a herd of cattle. This informant also corroborates Goodwin's statement that tag-band chiefs often were mere figureheads, set up by the government.

Apparently, even when the government issued cattle to the Indians with the idea of starting individual herds, these animals often served as ration beef. An elderly Apache man referred to this situation when he said:

> "Cattle were first issued in 1884. Five head to each family head. They were a black beef cattle. But most Indians slaughtered the cattle right away. My family didn't. Indians could draw either beef rations or live cattle – my family took live cattle. Next cattle issued were Durhams, but they were mean cattle."

Thus we see the ration system as the starting point for the cattle herds of some of the Indians on the San Carlos Reservation.

According to statements in several annual reports the issuing of rations for the entire reservation population at San Carlos ceased in 1904. Annual reports indicate that subsequent to that year rations were issued only to indigent Indians, and to members of the tribal police force and the judges of the tribal courts. Superintendent McCray, in an article in the *American Cattle Producer* (1941:5), stated briefly the relation of ration goods to Apache subsistence and the changes which took place in the period following the cessation of rations.

> Most of the Indians lived on rations issued by the government. Their diet was supplemented by nuts, berries, and game procured through their own efforts. They derived some income through the sale of cordwood and wild hay to the government. By 1905 the Apaches began to find work off their reservations. . . . Within a few years most of the able-bodied Indians were finding seasonal employment away from the reservation.

3 WHITE CATTLE OPERATORS IN THE SAN CARLOS AREA

With the final capture and imprisonment of Geronimo and his followers in 1886, active, organized resistance on the part of the Apaches came to an end. Prior to this time, white cattlemen had developed ranches to whatever extent was possible in view of the continuing raids. Now that the raiding was over, the cattle-raising business fairly exploded through the eastern and southeastern portions of Arizona and the adjacent areas of New Mexico. Many of the cattle outfits were huge operations, grazing thousands of head of cattle. Expansion called for more and more grazing land; no opportunity was overlooked.

Initiation of Lease-Grazing

In 1938 the Soil Conservation Service prepared a report on the natural resources of the San Carlos Reservation, the history of their usage, and recommendations for their future development and use. One of the points made was that the reservation area was not sufficient to provide an adequate subsistence by hunting and gathering for the number of Indians resident there in the 1880's and 1890's. The authors added:

> But the great reservation was good for one thing, and this the Whites were not long in discovering. It was good for grazing; it was better than good, it was the best. Early in the nineties the Chiricahua Cattle Company quietly obtained, through the commissary department of the army post at old San Carlos, permission to graze a herd of 2,000 cattle on the Ash Flats to the east of the Triplet Mountains (1938:35).

The superintendent's annual report of August, 1892, states that several thousand head of cattle belonging to the Sierra Bonita Land and Stock Company, faced with starvation on their own range, "had been allowed to graze upon the Indian lands." This had the sanction of the Department of the Interior and, subject to payment, "many of the cattle had been grazing on the Indian pastures without interference." The cattle companies apparently considered it their right, for the superintendent continued, "In my opinion a number of these ranges were located with the view of such grazing on the Indian lands. . . . the cattle came in from all directions." The situation became so bad that troops were called on to round up the unauthorized cattle and run them off the reservation ranges. The sum of $2,517 was collected from the Sierra Bonita Company.

The report of July, 1893, also mentions the encroachment of cattle on reservation lands due to drought conditions. The superintendent then added that

> I respectfully submit that it might prove of advantage to establish a system of leasing the Indian pasture lands, which are not used by the Indians, for grazing of citizens' stock. As matters are now it is an utter impossibility to prevent trespassing upon the reservation owing to its great extent.

In the annual report dated August, 1895, the superintendent commented that since his staff had been unable to keep outside cattle off the reservation, the department "authorized in September of last year the collection of a grazing tax for cattle running on the reserve." He added, "Doubtless there are many cattle whose owners do not pay for them." For the nine-month period $4,000 had been collected, and these funds were used to purchase a gristmill and to buy some stallions.

A major factor involved in the inability of Indian Service personnel to control grazing on the San Carlos Reservation around the turn of the century was the fact that there were no boundary fences. With White cattle outfits operating immediately adjacent to the reservation it was practically impossible to keep cattle from drifting onto reservation land. As mentioned above, the superintendent stated in his report of 1892 that it was his opinion that White cattle outfits had located their operations so as to take advantage of grazing on reservation lands. Apparently, many cattle owners considered this to be their right. If this opinion was correct, there probably was little, if any, effort made by the cattle companies to keep their livestock off the reservation.

History of Lease-Grazing

The early history of lease-grazing on the San Carlos Reservation is not clear on the basis of records available during this study. As mentioned previously, the Soil Conservation Service Report of 1938 states that in the early 1890's the Chiricahua Cattle Company quietly secured permission to graze two thousand head of cattle on Ash Flat. The same report goes on to state:

> In 1899 an intelligent half-breed Indian, son of one of the first White traders, protested that their [permittees'] cattle were encroaching upon the grounds where he was trying to raise a few himself. (When he inquired of the white outfit who gave them permission, he was told to mind his own business. He proceeded to do this.) Subsequent investigation showed that the Chiricahua Company was running 12,000 instead of 2,000 head. Rather than move off, the "Three C's Outfit" agreed to a lease paying a nominal fee per head.
>
> On the face of it, it was a wise and easy, if partial, solution of the problem of how San Carlos Indians were to eat. More and more big "Cow Outfits" moved in, the Double Circle, Bar-F-Bar, Cross-S, the Bryce-Mattice.

During the years that lease-grazing was in effect on the San Carlos Reservation there were a number of increases in the grazing rate. It has been impossible to determine, on the basis of available information, the year in which each increase took place; however, the following list indicates the rates in effect in specific years.

Year	*Rate per Head*	
1892	$ .50	
1903	1.00	
1912	1.40	
1915	2.00	(For excess over permitted number, regular fee plus 25% penalty fee.)
1921	2.40	for cattle
	3.00	for horses
1923		Cattle – 7% of average price locally Horses – cattle charge plus 20% Burros – half the charge for horses
1924	1.75	for cattle
	2.10	for horses

However, the mere fact that the permittees agreed to the grazing fees established by the government did not mean that subsequent relationships were smooth and pleasant. There was, in addition, the matter of the number of head of cattle and horses to be grazed on the reservation on any particular permit. The superintendent's annual report for 1913 says:

> In former years it was a common practice on the part of certain non-residents to turn cattle on the reservation for grazing purposes, and run them off again at opportune times. The policy of maintaining surprise round-up has been discouraging and expensive to these chronic and wilful trespassers, who in consequence are violently opposed to the present Superintendent.

At the time this study was made, there were in the agency office at San Carlos files entitled "Leasing of Lands – Permittees," with separate folders for certain of the permittees. One of these permittees will be designated here as Company R. The first item in one of the files pertaining to this company is a letter dated December 12, 1906, concerning the collection of the sum of $302 assessed against the permittee who grazed more head of stock on the reservation than the permit stipulated. In this same file, for each year from 1911 to 1917 inclusive, there was an exchange of correspondence between some government official and the permittee regarding livestock on the reservation in excess of the permitted number. During these years the permits for this company allowed an average of twenty thousand head of cattle and horses per year. During these same years the excess over the permitted number of head was stated to be between five thousand and eight thousand. The number in excess was declared by the permittee in an affidavit. During most of this period the government did not have the personnel to count the number of head actually being grazed on the reservation by any one permittee. In a few instances where the amount of excess declared in the affidavit was checked by an actual field count the number of excess head of livestock on the reservation was found to be considerably greater than the number stated in the affidavit. Some of the letters that were exchanged concerning the number of excess stock and the charges made for them include statements couched in rather strong language.

To relieve the hostile relationships existing between Indian Service officials and the permittees, the superintendent of livestock for the western part of the country made the following recommendation in 1917:

> In order that an accurate report of the count and the number of calves branded may be procured, a stockman, competent to handle such work properly, should be detailed to accompany the roundup outfits of all the permittees at the time such work is being carried on.

A case in point is the following statement made in 1917 by the superintendent at San Carlos in a letter to the Commissioner of Indian Affairs. The statement concerns Company R.

> I feel that these people have and keep a very close count of their stock; but, as I above stated, insist that our range-count alone be the basis of their affidavits. On some San Carlos ranges, we know that cattle were driven at night to escape the next morning's count; but these tactics were practically abandoned when it was seen that we were determined in getting a good count.
>
> If we accomplish raising this cattle business to a fair and open business transaction, it will be worth all of our trouble and effort.

In a determined effort to secure the real facts, this superintendent, in the same year, wrote to the county assessor at Globe for livestock statements from this company for the years 1911 through 1917. He said that this request was made "for purpose of aiding in settling a dispute as to amount of excess stock this company has on the Indian Reservation."

Correspondence in the files concerning another cattle company, referred to here as S, points up certain other difficulties in the relationships between the government and the cattle owners.

In some instances, one man – sometimes two or more – would be an officer in two companies. If there were an excess of livestock on the range of one company, he would claim the right to cover this by a shortage on the range of the other company. To add to the confusion, in situations of this kind, the names of the companies, while different in actual wording, were very similar.

In the file concerning Company S there is a letter from an officer of that company to the superintendent of the reservation concerning an excess of 1041 head of cattle on Range (X). The officer says: "Now in reply I want to say these cattle, the most of them, came from across the imaginary line from Range (Z)." The two ranges were adjoining areas. Furthermore, certain men were apparently officers in both companies.

Statements by the field personnel of the Bureau of Indian Affairs point up certain practices of the White cattle outfits in regard to the location of their ranges in relation to the Apache reservations. These outfits had:

(1) adjoining ranges on the same reservation

(2) adjoining ranges on the San Carlos and Fort Apache reservations

(3) adjoining ranges on the San Carlos Reservation and adjacent national forests

It is obvious that since there were generally no fences around either the Indian reservations or the national forest reserves, livestock could drift back and forth across the imaginary boundaries on their own, or under pressure. Further evidence of this type of problem can be seen in the historical sketches of the ranges, provided later in this chapter. See particularly the sketch of Range E.

In general, relations between Company S and the government seem to have been good. The references in the files to excess stock on the range indicate that the penalty fees were paid without protest. However, the fact remains that there was an excess.

In 1918, Company S apparently transferred part of its grazing area to another company, to be referred to here as T. There is a letter in the file, for the same year, from Company T asking for a government representative to count livestock as it engaged in roundup work. Another letter later the same year asks for government assistance in rounding up trespassers' cattle on the Company T range.

In addition to the matter of trespass cattle on their ranges, White cattle outfits had to cope with the age-old problem of cattle rustling. This got so bad that one company officer proposed hiring detectives to ferret out the culprits. Apparently this was agreeable to the government and to the larger permittee outfits, except for Company R. There is in this file a letter from an officer of Company T to the superintendent agreeing to share the cost of hiring the detectives, and complaining about the attitude of Company R on this matter. Correspondence of slightly later date indicates that Company R did finally agree to share the detective costs on an area basis. Presumably the detectives were hired, but the available records do not indicate what happened in this matter.

At the time of this study, files were available in San Carlos for only two additional livestock companies. Both were somewhat smaller companies than the three discussed above. There is relatively little correspondence concerning these two companies, but what there is shows that relations with the government were good, with no disputes involved.

Apparently the various ranges on the San Carlos Reservation were first designated by number and later on by letter. Just when this change took place is not indicated in the available records. A map of the reservation dated 1910 shows sixteen ranges bearing numbers, and the Indian Cattle Range which was located along the Gila and San Carlos rivers (see Map 1). In the annual report for 1913 there is a list of permittees (see below), showing the number of the range, or ranges, occupied by each one.

A partial list of permittees, dated July 17, 1916, refers to the ranges by means of capital letters. Subsequent mention of the ranges is in terms of letters. This change from numbers to letters in designating the ranges took place then sometime between 1913 and 1916.

The files concerning permittees on the San Carlos Reservation show relatively few lists of permittees. Such lists must surely have been included in the annual reports of the superintendents, but not many were present in the files available at the time of this study. What appears to be the only complete list of permittees found during this study is a part of the superintendent's annual report for 1913.

Range	*Permittee*	*Range Capacity*	*Annual Rental*
1	Shanley Cattle Company	1,000	$1,400.00
2	Coburn Brothers	1,150	1,600.00
3	Coburn Brothers	300	510.00
4	Champion Cattle Company	500	700.00
5	W. C. and Zee Hayes	1,000	1,525.00
6	Robinson and Young	1,150	1,610.00
7	L. C. Hayhurst	250	350.00
8	John A. McMurren	500	757.50
9	Henry S. Boice	20,200	28,280.00
10	Double Circle Cattle Co.	13,600	19,040.00
11	G. A. Bryce	1,300	1,820.00
12	L. E. Brocker	1,660	2,324.00
13*	Eagle Creek Cattle Company	300	420.00
13*	Cromb and Wilson	300	420.00
14	Prina and Martin	300	429.00
15	R. P. Brooking	40	56.00
16	Marshall and Foster	500	700.00
		44,050	$61,951.50

**Two companies occupied the same range.*

It would be logical to include at this point a comparative list showing the extent to which the numbered and lettered ranges correspond. Unfortunately, range A does not correspond to range 1, range B to range 2, and so on. There is so much confusion in this respect that no list is being presented here, but rather the reader is referred to Maps 1 and 2 showing the numbered and lettered ranges, so that he may see for himself the difficulty involved.

The next list of permittees is dated July 17, 1916, and shows the letter designations for the ranges.

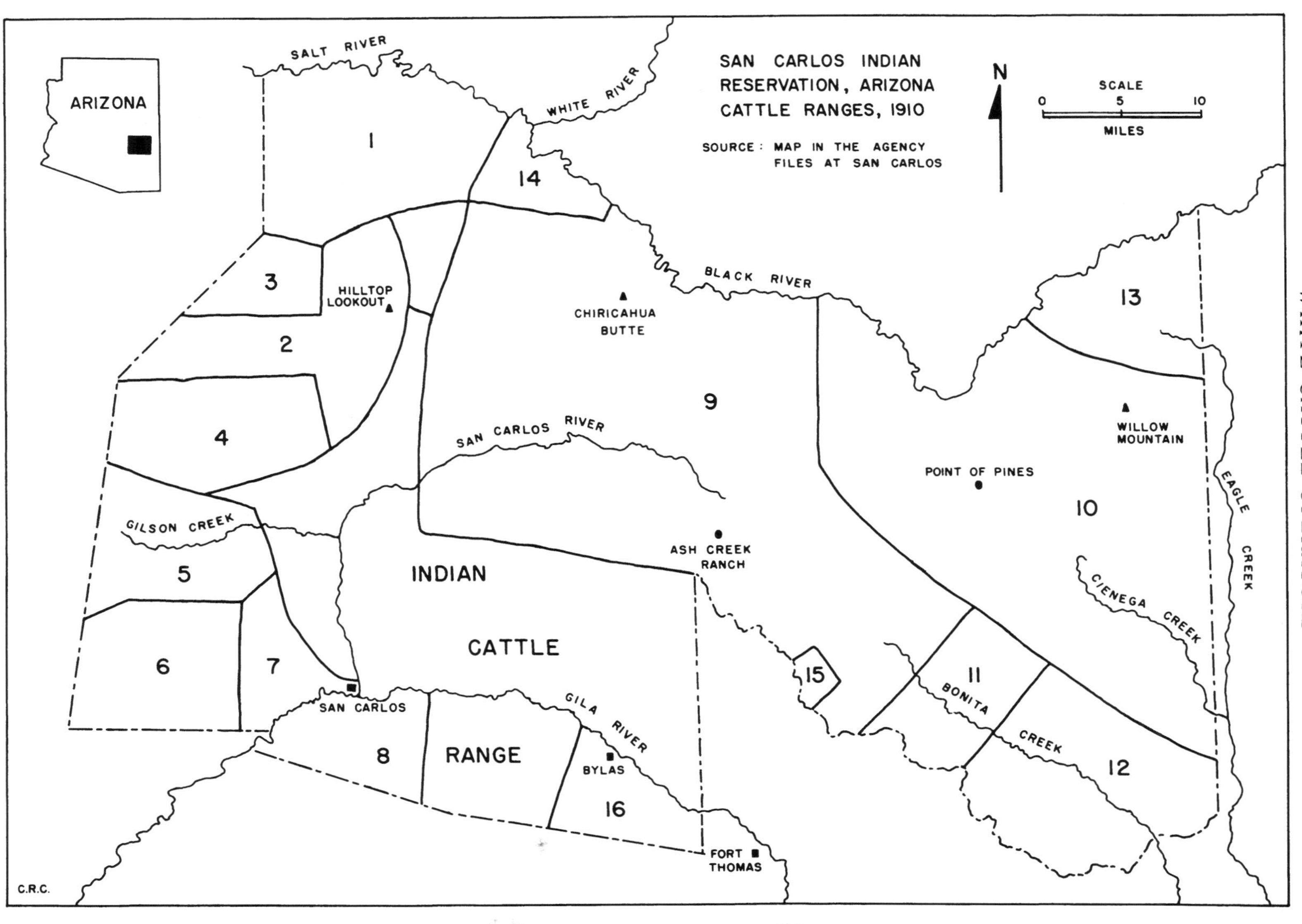

SAN CARLOS INDIAN
RESERVATION, ARIZONA
CATTLE RANGES, 1910
SOURCE: MAP IN THE AGENCY
FILES AT SAN CARLOS
N
SCALE
0 5 10
MILES
ARIZONA
SALT RIVER
WHITE RIVER
BLACK RIVER
EAGLE CREEK
CIENEGA CREEK
WILLOW MOUNTAIN
POINT OF PINES
BONITA CREEK
CHIRICAHUA BUTTE
HILLTOP LOOKOUT
SAN CARLOS RIVER
ASH CREEK RANCH
GILSON CREEK
INDIAN CATTLE RANGE
SAN CARLOS
GILA RIVER
BYLAS
FORT THOMAS
1
2
3
4
5
6
7
8
9
10
11
12
13
14
15
16
C.R.C.

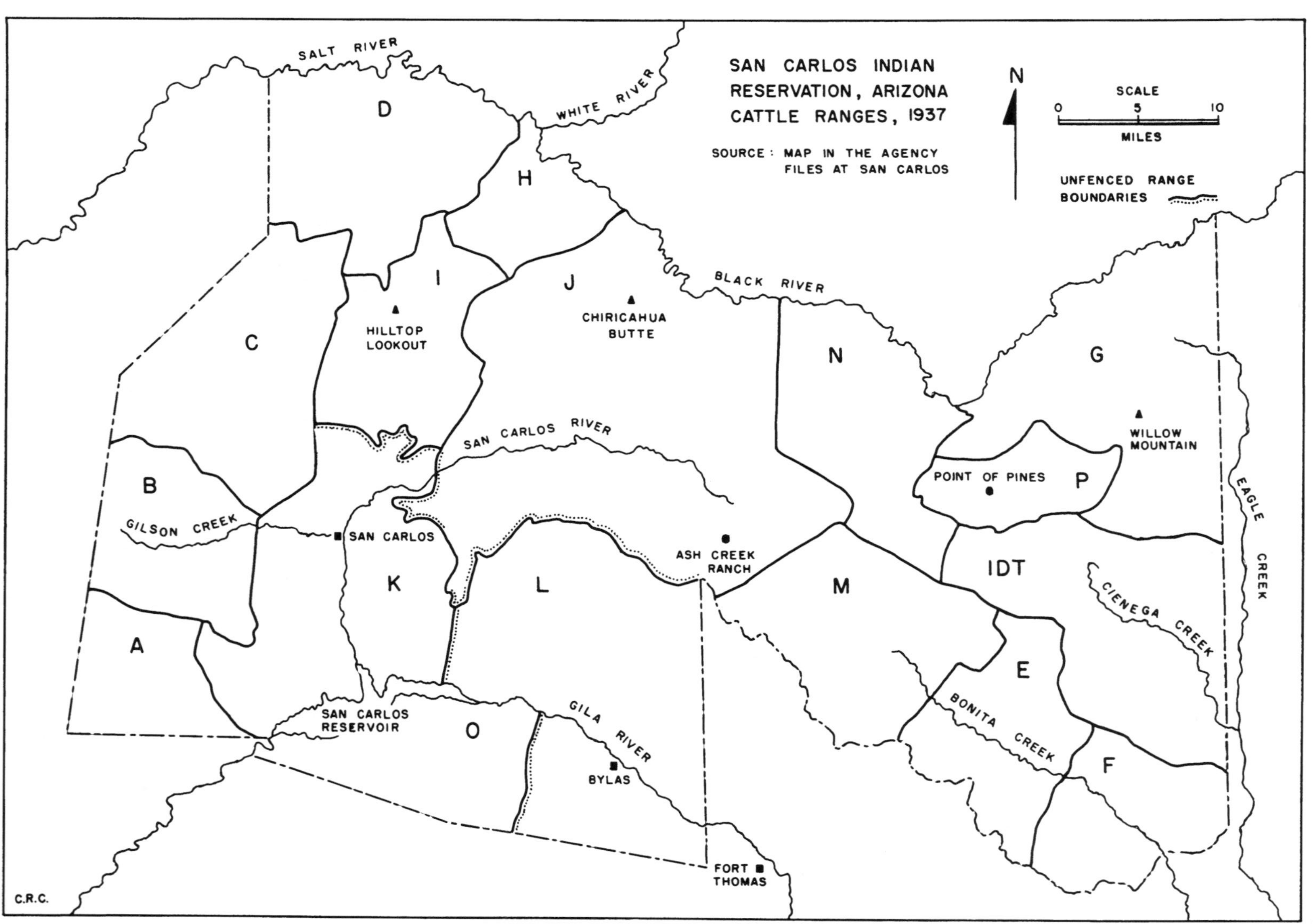
SAN CARLOS INDIAN RESERVATION, ARIZONA CATTLE RANGES, 1937
SOURCE: MAP IN THE AGENCY FILES AT SAN CARLOS
N
SCALE
0 5 10
MILES
UNFENCED RANGE BOUNDARIES
SALT RIVER
WHITE RIVER
BLACK RIVER
EAGLE CREEK
CIENEGA CREEK
BONITA CREEK
SAN CARLOS RIVER
GILA RIVER
GILSON CREEK
HILLTOP LOOKOUT
CHIRICAHUA BUTTE
WILLOW MOUNTAIN
POINT OF PINES
ASH CREEK RANCH
SAN CARLOS
SAN CARLOS RESERVOIR
BYLAS
FORT THOMAS
A
B
C
D
E
F
G
H
I
J
K
L
M
N
O
P
IDT
C.R.C.

Range	*Permittee*	*Range Capacity*	*Annual Rental*
A	Bar-F-Bar Cattle Company	1,150	$ 2,790.00
B	Missing	(missing)	(missing)
C	Coburn Cattle Company	no figures given	
D	H. G. Boice	20,500	49,500.00
E	G. A. Bryce	no figures given	
F	Bonita Cattle Company (Three Circle Cattle Co.)	2,050	4,950.00
G	Double Circle Cattle Co.	14,000	33,780.00
H	Drumm and Wilson	400	960.00

There is a list in the files dated January 11, 1921, which differs in that it provides the number of cattle and horses included in the permit. It does not give range capacity nor annual rental.

Range	*Permittee*	*Cattle*	*Horses*
A	J. N. Robinson	1,600	50
B	Zee Hayes	1,000	30
C	J. N. Robinson	4,700	250
D	H. G. Boice	20,000	500
E	G. A. Bryce	2,000	80
F	L. W. Samuels	2,000	50
G	John Landergin	14,100	300

The fourth list of permittees, showing the lettered ranges used by each one, is dated December 21, 1923. No additional data were provided with this list.

Range	*Permittee*
A	H.V. Roseberger (formerly Robinson and Young)
B	Zee Hayes
C	J. H. McVey (formerly Robinson and Young)
D	Chiricahua Cattle Company
E	Bryce and Mattice
F	L. C. Kelley
G	Double Circle

The Soil Conservation Service report of 1938 includes a summary of the history of lease-grazing on the reservation, as well as a brief historical sketch of each range, insofar as information was available. By the time the report was written, however, lease-grazing had been terminated and nearly all White permittees had vacated the reservation, groups of Indian cattlemen were in the process of organizing themselves into formal cattle associations, and the ranges were being designated by the names of the association or herd using each. These changes are discussed in detail in the next chapter.

In the section which follows, the general plan of the 1938 report is used. The statements presented are derived largely from this source, and, unless otherwise indicated, quotations are from the report.

Range A. This range, which formed the southwest corner of the reservation, corresponded fairly closely to the former Range 6, as the latter was shown on the 1910 map.

> Earliest data show that prior to 1910, Range A was used by Ben and Albert Gibson. . . .
>
> In the year 1910 Robinson and Young succeeded the Gibsons. . . . Robinson and Young continued to hold the range until 1921 when the Bar-F-Bar Cattle Company secured a permit on the area to range 1600 head of cattle and 100 horses. . . . it is a general opinion that many head were grazed in excess of the permitted number. This condition was very difficult to correct, as accurate counts were impossible due to unfenced and poorly fenced boundaries between National Forests, Public Domain and the Reservation.

Some of the information quoted above is not in agreement with data secured by this author from files at San Carlos. The list of permittees for 1913 does show Robinson and Young as using Range 6. However, the list for 1916 shows the Bar-F-Bar Company using Range A. Since the list of permittees for 1921 shows J. N. Robinson in possession of Range A, it is probable that there is an error regarding this range on the list for 1916.

> In the year 1922 the Bar-F-Bar Cattle Company was taken over by the Loan Company. Cattle and permit were taken. In 1925 the outfit was sold to G. L. Reay. . . .
>
> In 1927 the San Pasqual Land and Cattle Company bought the outfit. . . . This same company secured a permit on Range C and moved 1500 head from Range A to C. . . .
>
> In 1932, Mrs. Blake Hayes purchased the cattle on Range A. . . .
>
> In 1936, this range was taken from permit and retained for the use of the Tonto group of Indians. . . .
>
> Practically every outfit operating on Range A has lost money and cattle as a direct result of drought and overstocking.

Range A became a part of the area used by the Tonto Association. If the information quoted above is correct, then the H. V. Roseberger indicated as using Range A in 1923 may have been a representative of the loan company that took over from the Bar-F-Bar.

Range B. This corresponded fairly well to the former Range 5.

> As far back as records are available, Range B has been under permit to the Hayes family.
>
> . . . .
>
> The final permit terminates on May 1, 1938, but by agreement, the Hayes Livestock Company vacated Range B as of January 1, 1938.

This range lay immediately north of Range A, and also formed a part of the Tonto Association range.

Range C. This range apparently covered the area of former Range 3, and the western parts of 2 and 4.

> This range was used by Shanby Bros. prior to 1905.
>
> They branded ⋌ᕱ and +S and used what is now termed Ranges C and D. . . .
>
> Bob Sloan ran cattle on this area about 1906. Soon after this date, the range was acquired by Dennis Murphy, who branded the wine glass Ⲩ. Later Murphy sold to Coburn who occupied the range until about 1918, who later transferred it to Robinson and Young, who branded +S.

This apparently is largely in agreement with the permittee list of 1910. On that list, Coburn Brothers are shown as using Ranges 2 and 3, which were partially, at least, included in Range C. The name Shanby, shown above, is probably the same as the name Shanley shown on the 1913 list. The 1921 permittee list shows J. N. Robinson as using Range C, which agrees with the information quoted above.

> In the fall of 1923, Loan Company took the range and cattle. The permit was advertised and bid in by Hayes and Armstrong, who later merged into the San Pasqual Cattle Company.
>
> . . . .
>
> In 1933 they were notified to vacate the range around the Old Horse Camp for tribal cattle. The entire range was taken November 1, 1934 for Indian cattle. . . .

The permittee list of 1923 shows J. H. McVey as holding the permit. It is quite probable that he was a representative of the loan company. The foreclosures by loan companies on this range and on Range A in 1922 were apparently due to the fact that there had been severe drought conditions in 1921.

This range now largely comprises the area used until recently by the Circle Seven Association.

Range D. This range, in the northwest corner of the reservation, was formerly known as Range 1. The Soil Conservation Service report gives very little on the history of this range, not beginning until 1927. The 1913 permittee list shows the Shanley Cattle Company as using Range 1. On the 1916 list, the user of Range D is not shown. The 1921 list shows H. G. Boice, and the 1923 list the Chiricahua Cattle Company; these are essentially the same.

> Range C-2 was formerly a part of Range C and is now Range D. This range was taken from Range C.
>
> In 1927 this range was under permit to John Osborne for 2000 cattle and 50 horses. Mr. Osborne was notified in 1932 to vacate the range before 1934 in order to make it available for Indian owned cattle. . . .

Apparently Mr. Osborne was for a period of time the manager of the Chiricahua Cattle Company holdings on the San Carlos Reservation. So, perhaps this range continued essentially under Chiricahua control subsequent to 1927.

This range became the area used by the Hilltop Association.

Range E. Located in the southeastern part of the reservation, this was essentially the same as the former numbered-range 11.

> This range has been occupied for some forty years by Bryce and Mattice, who started in the cattle business on the public domain around Big Spring before there was any reservation fence. They grazed both public domain and the reservation. At that time there were no permits necessary for grazing on the reservation. When permits were required they obtained one. . . .
>
> . . . .
>
> None of these counts were very accurate, as the fence between the reservation range and public domain was left open in order that cattle on the reservation might utilize water just off the reservation on public domain, apparently an on and off agreement.

The above statements point up one type of difficulty — the lack of fences — that Indian Service field personnel faced in the administration of the lease-grazing permits.

The available lists of permittees bear out the point that the Bryce outfit had been in continuous possession of the permit for this range, from the time that permits were first required.

> It was in 1925 that Superintendent James B. Kitch first notified Bryce and Mattice that they would be expected to vacate their range for the expansion of Indian cattle, the approximate date set at 1927. However, in 1926, . . . other plans were made to let them remain for a while. In the year 1927 Mr. Mattice withdrew from the outfit.
>
> On November 1, 1932, a new permit was made to run until October 31, 1933. . . . At the expiration of this permit, Mr. Bryce was to vacate the range for Indian cattle use but failed to vacate until the Indians built a fence through the center of the range.
>
> In obtaining this range from the permittee for the use of the Indians for their own cattle, the San Carlos Agency experienced many disappoinments and setbacks. Extensions were granted with little regard to the wishes of the field men and the Superintendent, and at the time the personnel here did not know if the former permittee was trespassing or not, but the removal was finally made, and the Slaughter Mountain Cattle Association was formed by a group of approximately forty Indian cattle owners.

This quotation provides an excellent example of the problems the superintendent and his staff had to meet in removing the permittees and turning the ranges over to the Indian cattle owners. These problems involved resistance not only from the permittees, but also from the Washington office of the Bureau of Indian Affairs. In many such situations the field personnel were completely frustrated. As indicated above, this range was taken over by the Slaughter Mountain Association.

Range F. This range, in the southeast corner of the reservation, was the same as the former range number 12.

The Soil Conservation report states that "very little of the early history of this range is available." The 1913 permittee list shows this range under permit to an L. E. Brocker, the 1916 list shows the Bonita Cattle Company, in 1921 it was L. W. Samuels, and in 1923 it was L. C. Kelley.

> However, in the early days, the Hat outfit used it. They were succeeded by the Point of Pines. This remnant was sold by Mr. Kelley to J. M. Smith, who did not obtain a permit.
>
> Mr. Boyd Fury obtained a permit for 2000 cattle from 1928 to 1930, but due to inability to pay grazing fees the permit was cancelled in 1929.
>
> The above arrangement, whereas Mr. Smith owned the remnant of the Point of Pines cattle and Mr. Fury owned the permit, as on previous occasions where similar circumstances occurred, caused a great deal of conflict and court procedure.
>
> In 1929 the Double Circle Cattle Company obtained a permit for 2000 for one year, after which this permittee divided the permit, letting Lee Brothers bid on the south half.
>
> In 1929 Lee Brothers obtained a permit on the south half for three years on 5000 sheep. The Double Circle Cattle Company obtained a new permit on the north half for 1000 cattle. The Double Circle was moved off the north half in 1937 to make way for cattle belonging to a group of Indian cattle owners.
>
> The Lee Brothers now have a removal permit expiring May 1, 1938 and if the range is needed for Indian-owned stock at that time no further extension will be made.

This range had a rather varied history so far as the permit for its use is concerned. This may be due to the fact that in general it is very rough and rocky country. By 1954 the area was divided, part of it being used by the IDT herd, and the other part by the Slaughter Mountain Association.

Range G. This range formed the northeast corner of the reservation. It included roughly the area in the numbered range 10, and all of the range 13. It is all high country and is characterized by expanses of prairie land. The author of the Soil Conservation Service report gives some rather interesting historical facts regarding this area.

> Although no records are available for the very early history of this range, I am advised by Jim Stevens who is on the rolls of this Reservation, and who spent the early part of his life there, as to some of the early history.
>
> George H. Stevens, Commissary Sergeant in the United States Army, while on duty in the Forts, married an Apache girl. They settled on what is now the Double Circle Ranch headquarters about the year 1878. They ran cattle and sheep on what is now the entire east half of the reservation. There were no other settlers or stockmen in that portion of the country. In 1880 he sold his cattle to a man named Newlin but kept the sheep which he grazed until 1883. Numerous raids by Indian chiefs, Victorio and Geronimo, killing sheep and herders, caused Stevens to sell out his sheep.

Tom Newlin, who also had difficulties with these renegade chiefs, sold the cattle to Joe Hansen about 1883, and Hansen started the Double Circle brand.

The Double Circle changed hands occasionally, and when permits were required on the reservation, they obtained one on the San Carlos and one on the Fort Apache Reservations. They also ran cattle on the outside, east of the reservation.

. . . .

In 1934 the Indian Service requested the use of the west portion of the range for individual cattle. In 1934 a removal permit was written covering a two-year period for 2600 cattle and a fence built from the Point of Pines north and south, dividing the range into two parts; the west end which is now lettered N and the east which remains as G. [The removal permit was extended to November 1, 1937, and individual Indian cattle were moved on just as soon as the permit expired.]

The reference to the Double Circle Company having permits on both the San Carlos and Fort Apache reservations, as well as on land adjacent to both reservations, is further evidence of the difficulties that field personnel of the Indian Service encountered in administering the lease-grazing system. The difficulties remained even though the Double Circle and other outfits were very willing to cooperate with government officials.

On the 1913 list of permittees Range 10 was shown as permitted to the Double Circle Cattle Company, and Range 13 to the Eagle Creek Cattle Company. This author does not have information indicating whether or not these two companies were connected with each other in any way. On the 1916 and 1923 lists of permittees the Double Circle Company is shown as holding the permit for Range G. The 1921 list shows John Landergin as holding the permit, but this man may have been an official of the Double Circle Company, since the 1921 list shows only individuals and not the names of any companies.

This range, as first set up, was until recently divided about equally between the Point of Pines Association and the IDT Herd. That part which was set off as Range N was used by the Clover Association.

Range H. As pointed out in the Soil Conservation Service report, the history of Range H also involves Ranges J, I, and part of L. All comprised what had been known prior to 1938 as Range D.

Range H is a small range lying in the northwest part of the Reservation. The range is . . . mostly very rough. . . .

Ranges H, J, I, and part of L all formerly comprised Range D. About 1889 the Chiricahua Cattle Company obtained a beef contract to furnish meat to the Army Post at Fort San Carlos. They brought in about 2000 steers and obtained permission to run them on Ash Flat until they were all killed for beef. There were a few Indian-owned cattle there, and when the Chiricahuas became so numerous as to aggravate these individuals they reported to the commander at the Post, who upon investigation found that they were running around 12,000 cattle, many of which were she stuff. They were required to pay on that number. Around 1900 the outfit changed hands, and the Chiricahua name was dropped. In 1908, the Boyce, Gates, and Johnson Cattle Company succeeded the Chiricahua Cattle Company.

In December 1919 this company changed its name to the Chiricahua Cattle Company with Henry Boice as trustee. . . . In 1922 a small strip of about nine sections was withdrawn from Range D and given to Range E. . . . In 1925 the Indians took a portion of Ash Flat, reducing the permittee's number by 1000 head. The purebred pasture was taken in 1927 and another portion of the range around Warm Spring was claimed. . . . The last permit was from 1927 to 1930 . . . after which all of the range was used by Indian cattle. The Victor group now operates on a portion now known as Range H. The main portion is now known as Range J and the old steer pasture is known as Range M. Range I, however, was a portion taken about 1914 for use of the tribal herd.

It appears from past history that Range H was at one time a portion of a large range formerly known as Range D.

The Range D referred to above apparently included what had formerly been the numbered ranges 9, 14, 15, and parts of 1 and 10. Range 9 was a huge range (see Map 1). The 1913 list of permittees shows Henry S. Boice in control of this permit. In the 1916 and 1921 lists Range D is shown as being used by H. G. Boice, and in 1923 it was held by the Chiricahua Cattle Company. As far as it goes, the information from these lists of permittees seems to agree with the history of the name, Chiricahua Cattle Company.

The area included in Range H was the range used by the Victor Association.

The historical data cited above indicate that the Boice family, operating part of the time as the Chiricahua Cattle Company, gained a foothold on Ash Flat with the cattle for their beef contract, and then expanded west and north over a very large area of the reservation. This was also some of the choice grazing land on the reservation. Most of this great area was taken over by the Ash Creek Association, with portions being used by the registered herd, and by the Victor and Cassadore associations.

Range I. This range lay some distance due north of the present agency at San Carlos. It adjoined the old Range H on the southwestern boundary of the latter. The history of this range has been pretty largely covered in the discussion of Range H. It coincided largely with the numbered Range 2. "Range I was withdrawn from permit in 1914, it being one of the first ranges used in its entirety by Indians."

This range, as a whole, was used by the Cassadore Association.

Range J. This formed the major part of the old numbered Range 9, which was a great deal larger than any of the other numbered ranges.

Most of the history available for this range was given under Range H. It now forms the northern half of the range used by the Ash Creek Association.

Range K. This range, which extended northward from the Gila River on both sides of the San Carlos River, included the former Range 7, and the western part of the Indian Cattle Range as that area is shown on the 1910 map. It consists of lower elevations and generally semi-desert country.

> These ranges [K, L, and O] have been retained for the use of Indian stock . . . since the establishment of the Reservation. There have been a few attempts to let permits on these areas, but the Indians have persistently objected, causing non-issuance on these areas. Range K was added to by the withdrawal of the Chiricahuas, and little changes have been made other than the numerous withdrawals of land from the Reservation.
>
> Indian usage in the past has been heavy, many Indians living on the range and keeping their horses on the range year-long. . . .
>
> The range is assigned to the San Carlos Indian Livestock Association with a membership of fifty-eight owners. . . .

It may be that the San Carlos Indian Livestock Association referred to above is the general tribal association mentioned in some of the files for the period of the late 1920's and early 1930's. This general association is discussed briefly in the next chapter.

The Tin Cup Association occupied practically all of Range K.

Range L. As shown on the map of 1937, this corresponded to the large eastern portion of the Indian Cattle Range and Range 16, as these areas are shown on the 1910 map.

On the list for 1913, Range 16 was shown as being under permit to Marshall and Foster. The other historical data available in regard to this range are indicated in the quotation under Range K, above.

At present, this entire range is a part of the area used by the Ash Creek Association.

Range M. Lying immediately north of the Gila River, it consisted, for the most part, of rolling grassland country. For the history of this range, the reader should refer back to the statements regarding Range H. In addition, the report says that

> this range has been previously used as a community steer pasture, for the use of any range to hold their steers in, but the present plan is to build steer pastures on each range, thereby making Range M available for the exclusive use of the group on Range J. Range M will be used seasonally to hold steers in after the spring roundup starts, until sale time at the conclusion of the work and to hold the cut back cattle in until the fall sale, also to hold the sale cattle in during the fall roundup.

This author is unable to verify the fact that such usage was made of this range, however it was probably so used for a period of time prior to the establishment thereon of the purebred or registered herd. This range is used by the registered herd at present.

The area of this range is also known as the Ash Flat region. On the 1910 map it is shown as the eastern part of Range 9. The 1913 list shows Range 9 under permit to Henry S. Boice. The quotation given under Range H, above, showed that this is the grazing area where the Chiricahua Cattle Company secured permission to run 2000 head of cattle in 1889. It also stated that in 1925 the Indians took a portion of Ash Flat, and that the purebred pasture was taken in 1927.

Range N. This was the western portion of the former Range 10 as well as the former Range G. The statements quoted in regard to Range G indicate that in 1934 the Indian Service requested the use of the western part of Range G for the grazing of cattle owned by individual Indians. In that same year a north-to-south fence was constructed, setting off what became known as Range N from Range G.

The area of Range N was essentially the same as that later used by the Clover Association.

Range O. The 1937 map shows this range as located entirely south of the Gila River, south of Range K, and west of the southern portion of Range L. It was largely the same as the former Range 8, which the 1913 list shows as being under permit to John A. McMurren. As pointed out in the comments regarding Range K, this was one of the ranges generally retained for the use of the Indians. Later the Mohave Association used this range.

Range P. This is shown on the 1937 map as lying between Range G and the range for the IDT herd. No historical data about this range are available.

Map 1 shows some very peculiar sizes and shapes for the numbered ranges. Some of these ranges seem to have had no relationship to natural features – rivers, mountains, mesas, or prairie lands. Range 15 was the smallest of all. Why it was established as a separate range is a question. The 1913 permittee list shows it leased for 40 head of livestock. Eventually this range became a part of Range M. Another unusually small range, with no apparent relationship to natural features, was Range 14. Although not so small, Range 2 was an extremely peculiar shape – again without relationship to topography. Range 9, which was very large, could easily have formed three or four smaller ranges; or, if this was a reasonable size, then some of the smaller ones could have been combined.

Apparently, the lettered ranges, as first set up, included only A through G. Ranges D and G seem to have been very large areas which correspond roughly to the areas of the former Ranges 9 and 10, respectively. Ranges D and G were later broken up to form additional lettered ranges. Therefore, the map of 1937 shows ranges lettered up to, and including, Range P. However, as previously pointed out, no historical information concerning Range P is available.

As is shown in the next chapter, in some instances a single lettered range became the range used by an Indian cattle association. In other instances, two adjacent ranges were combined and used by an association.

Termination of Lease-Grazing

The Soil Conservation Service report of 1938 includes the following statements regarding the termination of lease-grazing:

> It seems that prior to the arrival of Mr. Kitch in 1923, there had been very little planning for the future welfare of the San Carlos Apache.
>
> . . . .
>
> Upon the arrival of Superintendent Kitch, he immediately took inventory of resources and made a study of the Indians and submitted a plan for the future of the Indians making them into an independent and self-supporting people.
>
> Superintendent Kitch recommended . . . that permits owned by White ranchers be terminated as the Indian cattle increased.
>
> Superintendent Kitch predicted that if the Office would give support to his plan that within fifteen years the Indians would have the entire range stocked with high grade Hereford cattle and would be selling more than 10,000 head per year.
>
> The Office finally agreed with the understanding that they would hold Mr. Kitch responsible for the success of the Plan.
>
> It seems that Mr. Kitch has carried out his plan very successfully and in a most satisfactory manner. . . .

Further on in the same report there are additional comments regarding the role of Mr. Kitch in terminating lease-grazing.

> He did a little quiet talking where talking counted, and in 1923 Charles H. Burke, then Commissioner of Indian Affairs said doubtfully,

"If you think you can do it, go on down there and try." [Referring to Kitch's transfer from Fort Peck Agency, Montana.] In September 1923 he arrived to become Superintendent of the San Carlos Reservation.

The barons were well entrenched. It had been a very soft thing and they were ready to fight for it. . . . They "went to Washington." But in the end "Washington" broke down in favor of the Indians – and because James Kitch battered the opposition down. The budget-makers, of course, succumbed to his persuasive figures, they liked the idea of self-support for Indians.

In 1924 they authorized him to order the Ash Flat Range vacated by Whites and returned to the Indians. He moved in 900 cows. His toe was in the door. Cross-S was next to go, then Bar F Bar, and Bryce-Mattice, and old Chiricahua of the ranches, and the last to go was Double Circle. They moved off this year, 1938. There remain two insignificant White holdings under special conditions.

A booklet, *San Carlos Hereford Feeder Sales,* published in 1948, contains a similar statement regarding the role of Mr. Kitch.

In the year of 1923, Mr. James B. Kitch came to San Carlos as Superintendent. Mr. Kitch proved to be a true friend of the Apache Indians. He also proved to possess enough nerve to face the politics and criticism of the white man and to champion and befriend the Apaches. Aided and encouraged by his stockman, Hiram E. Brown, . . . the leases were gradually cancelled and the ranges stocked with Indian cattle.

Superintendent McCray, writing to the Commissioner of Indian Affairs in 1941, commented:

When Superintendent Kitch took charge of this reservation nearly eighteen years ago . . . [he] knew, if the Indians would utilize their good grazing lands, the income of the reservation could be increased. With this in view, he began a systematic elimination of the white permittees. This process was opposed at every step. Not only the white stockmen fought being removed but the Indians accused Mr. Kitch of destroying their tribal income. Even the Indian Office questioned the wisdom of such a program. Indians refused to accept cattle individually and the Superintendent was forced to establish tribal herds to utilize the reclaimed ranges.

Mr. Kitch's feelings regarding the elimination of White permittees are indicated in the following statements taken from a letter that he wrote to the commissioner in 1933.

We appreciate the fact that the withdrawal of any range from permittee is one of our most unfortunate and unpleasant duties. We realize that the White people have for many years been privileged to partake of the advantages of Indian reservation grazing and we also appreciate the many thousands of dollars received in permit fees, but we must decide, if Indian protection is to be facilitated and if we are to properly conserve their range areas and build their cattle interests, that such advancement or what might be termed encroachment on White permittee rights must be made.

. . . .

We fully appreciate the inconvenience to these two permittees but we must also feel our sense of duty and obligation to the San Carlos Apache Indians who have gone on record, and I might say the first Indian reservation I have ever heard of which has taken such action in a self-sustaining program of support and administration.

It was Kitch who was able to put into operation the policy of terminating the grazing leases. Nevertheless, it should be pointed out that Superintendent Symons, in his report for 1921, recommended that "as fast as the Indian cattle need the range the White permittee should be crowded back and the Indian allowed the use of the range."

A man who was one of the field supervisors on the reservation during Kitch's period of office has said, in conversation, that Kitch was responsible for the development of the Indian cattle industry. "Indian cattle were running only along the river ranges. Kitch cancelled the leases and got the Indians to move onto the ranges as they were cancelled."

One Indian informant commented that "Kitch was a very good man. Interests outside the reservation, that is permittees whose leases Kitch wanted to cancel in favor of Indian stockmen, influenced some of the Indian cattlemen to write up a petition to the Indian Office requesting that Mr. Kitch be ousted because the Indians were losing the permittees' fees."

Referring to Kitch and his field assistant, Hi Brown, the stockman, another Indian informant said: "Mr. Kitch was well liked by all Apaches. And Hi Brown was the best cattleman we ever had on the Reservation."

Other Indian informants made similar complimentary comments regarding Kitch and Brown.

Most of them gave Kitch credit for terminating the grazing leases and putting the Indians in the cattle business. A few were inclined to give Brown more credit for the operation. However, both men seem to have been highly regarded by the Indians.

As leases were terminated, efforts were made to get groups of Indian cattle owners to take over and operate the vacated ranges. Writing to the commissioner in 1933, Kitch said: "It is our plan in taking over these permits to place a number of individual family groups within them. . . ."

Statements by Indian informants in general corroborate the office records regarding the beginning of lease-termination, and establishment of Indians on the ranges. One informant said that "until 1923 the Indians ran cattle just on the river range. In 1924 they took over Ash Flat from the Chiricahua Cattle Company."

Another Indian informant said that "when the Double Circle range was taken, Superintendent Kitch asked, not told, a group of families to run cattle on the Point of Pines range."

A third Indian informant verified these statements when he said: "In 1924 when the Chiricahua Cattle Company lease was cancelled, Indians moved from the river range up to Ash Flat."

Using the data from the historical sketches of the various ranges, it is possible to compile a list of the last permittees to occupy the ranges. The list includes the dates, usually approximate, when the last permittees vacated.

Range	*Last Permittee*	*Date Vacated*
A	Mrs. Blake Hayes	1936
B	Hayes Livestock Company	Jan. 1, 1938
C	San Pasqual Cattle Company	Nov. 1, 1934
D	John Osborne	1934
E	G. A. Bryce	1933 or 1934
F	North Half – Double Circle Cattle Company	1937
	South Half – Lee Brothers	May 1, 1938
G	Double Circle Cattle Company	Nov. 1, 1937
H	Chiricahua Cattle Company	
	Part of Ash Flat	1925
	Purebred Pasture	1927
	(Remainder)	1930
I	Chiricahua Cattle Company	1914
J	Chiricahua Cattle Company	1930
K	(Indian Cattle Range)	–––
L	(Indian Cattle Range)	–––
M	Chiricahua Cattle Company	1927
N	Double Circle Cattle Company	Nov. 1, 1937
O	(Indian Cattle Range)	–––

A meeting of the board of directors, Ash Creek Livestock Association.

4 INDIAN CATTLE OPERATIONS ON THE SAN CARLOS RESERVATION

Beginnings

The beginning of Indian cattle raising were indicated in the discussion of the ration system on the San Carlos Reservation. As early as 1878 some Indians on the reservation were accumulating the poundage due them in the weekly issue of beef and drawing live cattle instead. These animals were used as a basis for establishing herds of cattle. The annual report in 1878 states that "one Indian has already accumulated 43 head, and the total number owned by the Indians in June last was 521 stock-cattle and 760 sheep."

Since the files at the San Carlos Agency that covered the cattle industry on the reservation went back only as far as 1903, it was necessary to turn to elderly Indians for information regarding the early years of the Indian cattle operations. Unfortunately, only a few of those interviewed had any memory of the nature and extent of the Indian cattle industry in their youth.

Apparently as early as 1884 the government issued cattle to the San Carlos Indians with the idea that they would start or increase their individual herds. One elderly Apache man said: "Cattle were first issued in 1884. Five head to each family head. They were a black cattle. But most Indians slaughtered the cattle right away. My family didn't."

Another elderly man said: "Some Indians had cattle before 1900. They bought those cattle themselves. They put them on the river ranges." Another man, who said he was born in 1896, said he did not know when the Indians first raised cattle on the reservation, but that when he was a boy his father had some cattle on the river range. One of the younger men said that he had heard that Indians ran cattle along the river around 1900, but that "these were cattle they had gone out and bought."

One of the files in the offices at San Carlos covered the general subject of stock raising from 1908 to 1922. There was a memorandum in this file, dated June 8, 1910, stating that 18 bulls had been purchased and issued to the Indians. Another memorandum, dated two days later, stated that the Indian Office on the reservation had purchased 500 cows and issued them to 50 Indians, 10 head to each man.

The annual report of the superintendent for 1913 includes a reference to the issue of 500 cows and subsequent handling of them by the Indians.

> The stock is so widely scattered that it is well-nigh impossible to secure an accurate count. . . . There are on the reservation now fewer than 3000 horses of all classes. . . . There are about 790 head of cows and steers belonging to Indians. About three years ago 500 head of cattle were issued to Indians. But approximately half of these cattle can be rounded up at this time. A surreptitious slaughter of these animals has been going on, and some of it has been due to stern necessity – the need for food. The Indians are being told that they cannot expect the Government to give them more cattle until they can show an increase from those already issued to them. In the previous issue, certain Indians–many of them employees with fixed wages–were selected as the beneficiaries of this distribution. Those who got no cattle were, and are yet, dissatisfied. It is possible that some of the dissatisfied ones have contributed materially to the unauthorized slaughter.
>
> Future issues of cattle, in equity, should be to the Tribe as a whole, or each individual beneficiary should be required to perform labor on roads, ditches, or construction work in payment for the cattle he receives. In no other way can dissatisfaction be stopped.

Some of the elderly Indian men who were interviewed during this study bore witness to the fact that there was considerable dissatisfaction with the manner in which the cattle were issued in 1910. One of them said:

> "From time to time the Government bought cattle from white cattle outfits and issued them to Indians. Maybe they even got some from south of the border. About 1908 they brought in 500 head, and gave 10 to each of 50 men. These men were the ones who went along with the Government on everything. Neither my father or I got any cattle in this issue, we weren't in right. Some other times they did this."

The same annual report for 1913 pointed out some of the difficulties encountered in trying to develop the Indian cattle industry on the reservation.

> Great difficulty has been experienced in preventing the Indians from selling yearlings. . . . Stockmen and farmers are instructed to show them the advantage of keeping their beef stock for greater weight and higher prices. . . . The total number of marketed cattle, therefore, was 192 head, for which there was received an aggregate of $4,021.42, or an average of $20.50 per head. . . . During the year permits were issued to slaughter 155 head of cattle for local consumption. . . . The estimated value of all livestock on the reservation belonging to Indians is $57,200.

The report also indicated another type of difficulty:

> With all of the opposition, antipathy and "fleecing" the Indians meet off the Reservation (and sometimes on it) it is small wonder that he goes back to his aboriginal practices and hunts game – in the form of cattle belonging to somebody else.

The annual report for 1915 states simply that individual Apaches owned approximately 1500 head of cattle in that year. In the spring of 1918 the livestock supervisor counted 2200 head of cattle, "not including the steers they sold at that time."

In the file entitled "Stock Raising," a letter dated September 19, 1919, from Cato Sells, Commissioner of Indian Affairs, to Superintendent Terrell, includes the following statement:

> Some of the Indians on your reservation have quite a number of stock, and those whose circumstances will permit them to do so should be required to purchase from their own funds one pure bred bull for each twenty head of cows and heifers which they run on the range.

The annual report for 1920 indicates that it was the thought of the Indian Service that the majority, if not all, of the San Carlos Indians would become successful stock-raisers, since

> stockraising is the only possible means of livelihood within the reservation and a successful program has been installed and is being carried out.

Further evidence that this policy was official with the personnel of the Bureau of Indian Affairs is found in a letter, dated September 18, 1923 – shortly after Kitch assumed the post of superintendent at San Carlos – indicating the number of Indian cattlemen on that reservation.

> I find from the records in the office here that there are 285 Indians who own cattle. The greater number of these Indians are heads of families and I believe represent at least one-half of the Indians of this reservation.

A few days later, Superintendent Kitch wrote to the commissioner that

> there are approximately 2500 head of cattle owned by the individual Indians. . . . We find between 250 and 300 Indians now interested in the cattle industry and it is the intention by the issuance of heifers from the tribal herd to interest as many more as possible and ultimately to bring these Indians all into the cattle industry.

A letter from Kitch to the commissioner, dated December 14, 1923, indicates his determination to get the Indians on the San Carlos Reservation into the business of raising cattle.

> I do not find the proper attention having been given the individual Indian cattle by the stock administration of this office, it being almost entirely diverted to the tribal herd. . . . I find a large number of Indians without any cattle whatsoever and in the future instead of issuing heifers to those already possessing cattle, they will be issued to those Indians who are worthy of help and who have less than five cows or heifers and in this way spread cattle ownership over a large number of individual Indians rather than the building up of individual herds of a few.

Kitch apparently carried out vigorously his program of expanding the cattle industry among individual Indians, for in a letter to the commissioner in March, 1926, he said, "During the past two years we have placed over 1400 head of she stuff with the Indians and this year will issue 700 more."

Apparently the cattle raised by the San Carlos Indians were steadily improving in quality, since Kitch reported in a letter dated May 7, 1926, to the commissioner that

> much favorable comment was made by the bidders at our sale on the quality of the Indian cattle. . . . We are very much pleased with the sale as herewith reported and especially in view of the fact that not only has it almost doubled previous sales but for the first time it has even topped or classed up with the sales of white herds in this section.

In May, 1927, replying to an official inquiry from Washington regarding the status of the cattle industry on the San Carlos Reservation, Kitch said:

> In our spring roundup just completed we actually counted or tallied 5527 head of she stuff over one year of age. . . . We have approximately 350 Indian families having cattle, 306 brands selling cattle last year. . . . Heifer calves from the tribal herd are sold to the Indians in small herds of twenty each under a five year reimbursable plan. . . . It will be seen that not only have cattle doubled by actual count in the past three years but that it is entirely self-supporting paying its own expenses besides paying a balance or profit into the tribe. . . .

In reply to an inquiry concerning roundup practices, Kitch, in July, 1927, mentioned the four regional roundup wagons, and went on to say:

> The men working the tribal herd and the wagon bosses of the Indian wagons [2] are paid from the tribal funds. This money coming from the sale of steers. . . . You will note that the Indian cattle in both the Bylas and the Rice wagons are managed by Indians. This is our method of training them to handle cattle themselves and I believe they are as capable of handling a wagon as well as any white man. . . . We are placing about thirty families in the cow business per year.

Foreshadowing developments in years to come regarding the matter of paying the expenses of handling – roundup and selling – of cattle owned by individual Indians, the commissioner, in a letter dated May 18, 1928, proposed "to find funds to pay the expenses of running the individual-owned stock . . . it would seem that the most practicable way would be to assess each head a certain amount. . . . "

A few years later, in a letter dated April 20, 1932, to the commissioner, Kitch summarized the Indian livestock situation at San Carlos at that time:

> It is noted that the cattle industry has been built up in nine years from approximately 2700 head of individually owned cattle . . . to approximately 16,000 head. . . . With approximately 600 brands, which is increasing annually by the sale of reimbursable heifers to new owners. I cannot but feel that the cattle industry is felt by each and every individual Indian of the reservation in some way. In fact, I know of no families at present not in some way affected by cattle ownership, either directly or indirectly.

Apparently, Kitch fostered the development of an association of Indians owning livestock on the San Carlos Reservation. It is variously referred to in the files as the San Carlos Cattle Association, San Carlos Cattlemen's Association, San Carlos Stock Association, and the San Carlos Livestock Association. As early as May, 1926, Kitch wrote the commissioner that

> considerable interest is being shown in the cattle industry by these Indians – the San Carlos Cattle Association comprising the owners of this district being recently organized with approximately 50 signed up members. A meeting will be held in Rice in the near future for the organization in this district.

At the time of this study, one of the files in the agency office at San Carlos was entitled "Stock Raising, Cattle Associations, General," and covered the period from February 1, 1932, to June 30, 1938. The first item in this file, but bearing no date, was a copy of the charter and by-laws of the San Carlos Cattle Men's Association. It said in part:

> The object of this Association shall be for the protection and benefit of cattle owners among the Indians and the upbuilding of the individual herds. . . . Any person may join this Association providing he is a San Carlos Apache Indian and subscribes and agrees to the provisions of the following by-laws: . . .

These contain provisions regarding attending roundups in person or by representative; butchering; not running cattle unnecessarily; branding calves; distribution of bulls; keeping up reimbursable sales; officers – president, secretary, and a range representative.

Writing somewhat at length to the commissioner in May, 1933, Kitch outlined some aspects of the Indian cattle industry, and the relations of the stock association to the operations.

> Nine years ago a roundup was simply a congregation of all classes and types of Indians and horses of approximately 600 pound pony stock and more or less an open holiday under the total responsibility of White employees. Numerous men gathered at the wagon for no other purpose than to be there and eat. . . . Under our organization plan of individual management these roundups have been developed under the immediate direction of the Indians themselves. Meetings would be held in the districts in which roundup bosses and those in authority would be selected and this has developed into the San Carlos Stock Association in which the entire roundup management is in the hands of officers representing each district. These men serve without pay unless acting as wagon bosses and are actually learning range management and the handling of stock. . . . A collection of $5 from all cattle sold is kept separate from any other funds and used exclusively in subsistence of these roundups and the employment of such Indians as are absolutely necessary – such as the cooks and other camp help above noted. I further feel . . . that additional positions of stockmen be Indians and that in selecting such employees that care be exercised not only as to their range ability but as to their leadership. In other words, I believe our employment of Indians in the cattle industry should be in a sense of a training school. . . . Officers of the Stock Association pass on all questions of brands, ownership of calves and the actual sale of these cattle. This year . . . will permit fifteen new Indians to engage in the cattle business. These selections will be made in proportion to the population in the San Carlos and Bylas districts by the officers of the Livestock Association which really places the entire industry in their hands.

It is doubtful that Kitch was really able to place the entire cattle industry in the hands of the association. Under subsequent reservation administrations this goal was not achieved – at least the operations of the Indian cattle industry were not carried on entirely by the Indians themselves.

On May 19, 1933, one of Kitch's staff members wrote to the commissioner regarding "a joint resolution to be presented to the Office by the Indian Business Committee, acting for the Tribe, and by the San Carlos Stock Association, acting in behalf of the individual cattle owners."

It has so far been impossible to determine either how long this general association existed, or why it ceased to operate. It is quite possible that the increasing number of cattle owners made the general, over-all type of association an unwieldy organization. Or it may be that the majority of cattle owners were not interested in such an association, preferring to operate on an individual basis, or in terms of family groups. It is also possible that the newly-established Tribal Business Committee was tending to serve the same, or some of the same, purposes as the stock association did.

Several of the more elderly Apache men were asked about the San Carlos Livestock Association, and mention was made of the other variants of the name. Only two of those interviewed remembered anything about such an association, and neither of those two had been members of the organization.

The annual report for 1935 indicates that the reservation cattle were under the supervision of three White stockmen.

> One white stockman is stationed in the field at Ash Creek Ranch, approximately 27 miles east of San Carlos, and the superintendent of livestock is stationed at Hill Top approximately 24 miles north of San Carlos. This latter employee has charge of the tribal herd, a portion of the registered-foundation herd, and supervises 3500 Indian cattle in this district. The Ash Creek stockman has approximately 10,000 head of individual Indian cows and 300 registered cows for foundation herd. . . . One white stockman, supervising the lower or river cattle, approximately 2000 head, is also stationed at San Carlos.

Desirable though it might be, it is practically impossible to provide a table showing the number of head of cattle on the San Carlos Reservation year by year. For some years no figures are available. For other years only one total is given, and it is not made clear whether or not that figure includes both individually-owned and tribally-owned cattle. The quotation above from the 1935 annual report is a case in point. It would appear that there were 13,500 Indian-owned cattle. It is also reasonable to assume that the 2000 head of river cattle were Indian-owned, since the registered herd was being grazed on the pastures on Ash Flat. But there is no indication as to how many head of cattle composed the "registered-foundation herd."

A letter from Kitch to the commissioner in March, 1937, states that there were 33,000 head of cattle on the reservation, and mentions the problem of personnel to handle them. Kitch had reported in 1932 that there were 16,000 head on the reservation. One wonders whether or not the cattle population would have doubled in five years considering all the normal losses – deaths, fluctuating calf crops, sales, and slaughtering.

Two items covering approximately the same period of time give further evidence of the confusion regarding the number of head of cattle on the reservation at any one time.

The 1938 Soil Conservation Service report says that "530 Indian 'cattlemen' now own 25,000 cattle. . . ." But in an article in the *American Cattle Producer* for October, 1941, Superintendent McCray wrote that "on June 30, 1938, there were 402 Indian cattle owners, with an average of 45 head of cows each, or approximately 18,000 head."

Nevertheless, in commenting on the problem of handling the 33,000 reported in 1937, Kitch said:

> To accomplish this administration, we have four stockmen. Previous to this when the reservation was under permit to whites, this same area, with practically the same number of cattle, was handled by seven permittees, each having a separate manager drawing up to $5,000 per annum with a bonus. Each of these outfits carried annually from five to twenty paid white cowboys. We are now operating this range with four stockmen and about six Indian lineriders supplemented by gratis assistance during roundups by the Indians.

Thus, in 1937 – and possibly earlier – we see the establishment of a pattern in the handling of reservation cattle that was destined to become a serious weakness in the years ahead. This 1937 pattern consisted in part of insufficient personnel to handle the cattle properly, and in part the fact that the personnel were to a great extent white men. Were the Indians really learning the cattle business? Were they *interested* in learning the cattle business? In 1933, Kitch himself had pointed out the danger of such a pattern developing when he wrote to the commissioner:

> The great danger in cattle expansion is the possibility of too much Government control and management with the resulting effect upon the Indian that he will become a dividend receiver rather than an actual owner and participant in his own industry. I believe the location of family groups or clan groups within already fenced areas will develop their personal industry and interest.

Establishment of Range Groups

In the quotation above, Kitch was announcing a principle regarding the San Carlos cattle industry which he firmly maintained in succeeding years. It was his conviction that the Indian cattle industry should be organized in terms of family or clan groups.

However, before he could realize his goal of establishing the San Carlos Indians in the cattle business Kitch had to overcome some serious obstacles. As pointed out previously, Kitch was opposed by practically everyone – White permittees, Indians, and the Indian Office in Washington. Probably the most difficult job he had was convincing the Indians that the income derived from the White permittees would be more than balanced by the income from the expansion of their own cattle industry. Superintendent McCray in a letter written in 1941 pointed out that after Kitch was successful in his campaign to remove White permittees from the grazing areas on the reservation, "Indians refused to accept cattle individually, and the Superintendent was forced to establish tribal herds to utilize the reclaimed ranges." In his article in the *American Cattle Producer* (1941:5), McCray further pointed out that "many of the Indians were hesitant, as the purchase of a few heifers obligated them to be on hand for roundup work and immediate income impossible."

McCray's last point indicates one of the problems that generally confront the advocates of directed culture change. Any instance of directed culture change which requires the expenditure of effort over a long period of time before benefits are achieved is very difficult to promote successfully. In the cattle industry, for instance, real success requires consistent effort over a relatively long period of time.

In a letter dated September 18, 1923, to the supervisor-in-charge at San Carlos, the western supervisor of livestock recognized a problem that still remains as one of the most serious handicaps to the successful operation of the San Carlos cattle industry, and which is discussed more fully in a later chapter. The livestock supervisor said:

> Efforts have been made to get some of the Indians along the Gila interested in what is known as the "Point of Pines," and while this is a beautiful country, good grass, shallow water, an abundance of fine timber, and might be farmed, and is an ideal stock country, still I think we are wasting our time trying to get an Apache to move there. Point of Pines is a very isolated country, being about 80 miles from the Agency, and the most of the way over the roughest kind of a dim trail.

In regard to the early efforts to remove permittees and establish Indian cattle owners on some of the better reservation grazing land, the supervisor of livestock for the western area said in a letter to the commissioner dated November, 1923:

> We all agree that in order to make a success of the Indian cattle industry it will be necessary to take over a part of some other range. . . . We have conferred with Mr. Kitch and all of the stockmen on these matters and we have finally concluded that the east or southeast end of the Chiricahua range would be best suited for the Indian cattle. . . . These Indians have always clamored for this Ash Flat country for their cattle.

Historical data regarding the various ranges, as given in the Soil Conservation Service report of 1938, indicate that in 1925 a portion of the Ash Flat range was taken from the Chiricahua Cattle Company and used as a grazing area for Indian-owned cattle. This is further confirmed by a letter, dated March 15, 1926, from Kitch to the commissioner, which includes the statement that the acquisition of 60 additional pure-bred bulls "will permit us to take a number of the tribal herd bulls and place them with the Indian cattle on Ash Flat."

Two additional letters from Kitch to the commissioner during 1926 indicate further developments in the organization of the Indian cattle industry. In one letter written in May of that year, mention is made of three roundup wagons working the Indian cattle at San Carlos, Bylas, and Ash Flat. Another letter written in October of that year states in regard to the fall sales: "You will note in these prices the increase paid on the Indian cattle, which were raised on Ash Flat and the cattle from the Tribal pasture over the desert or river cattle." A similar letter written in July, 1927, lists the three roundup wagons mentioned above, and an additional one referred to as the "IDA or Tribal." And in a letter written in May of 1927 Kitch remarked that "we have approximately 350 Indian families having cattle, 306 brands selling cattle last year."

The primary interest here is in the manner in which the Indians were organized into range groups. With this in mind it is important to note a statement included in a lengthy letter from Kitch to the commissioner, dated May 1, 1933:

> It is our plan in taking over these permits to place a number of individual family groups within them making in a sense small companies which will take over the same areas or in the same manner as formerly held by White permittees. I believe the only proper administration of the cattle industry, due to the fact that it will ultimately reach over 30,000 head, is the breaking up into small family groups or what might be termed company holdings with the encouragement that the Indians owning cattle in these areas will move with them.

The opening phrase above, "It is our plan in taking over," would seem to indicate that this was an action yet to come. Also the phrase "which will take over" lends support to the idea that the small companies had not really been established as yet. As pointed out previously, Kitch's hope and desire that "the Indians owning cattle in these areas will move with them" has not been realized to this day. The mention of the livestock association in the letter just referred to, as well as mention of the same organization in another letter written by Kitch later in the same month, definitely indicates that the general organization was still operating, and that the small associations were not yet in existence.

However, in a letter dated June 14, 1934, to an official of the Bureau of Indian Affairs, Kitch said:

> I further recommend that, where we are able to designate company areas such as Victor area on Black River now composed of 14 members, the Stephens [*sic*] area in the east end of Ash Flat which will with present plans contain 14 members, and the 38 individuals who are taking over the Circle 7 range, and those individuals who take over the John Osborn permit, these Indians working their own cattle within their own company permits be permitted to dispose of their mavericks or branding among themselves in their own discretion. These company groups are different from the large community herds in that they will have company management and company operation.

In the files available at San Carlos at the time of this study, the above statement was the earliest one indicating that Kitch was getting "company groups" of Indian cattle-owners established.

In 1937 Goodwin wrote a report on the status of the Indians on the San Carlos Reservation. This report, which was submitted to the Bureau of Indian Affairs, remains unpublished. In commenting on the Indian cattle industry he referred to the range groups in existence in 1935.

> In 1935 five or six bodies of cattle owners had range assignments of their own. Each of these was headed by one influential man, the recognized leader in the enterprise. The largest of these range assignment bodies is one composed entirely of White Mountain Apache from the Bylas district, numbering some 25 cattle owners. I understand the enrollment may go on increasing till their quota of 40 is reached. Their range is entirely within old White Mountain territory. Another body was assigned range in the region of Casador Springs, the head man considering he had a claim to it as his father's local group in pre-reservation times resided in the area. When range is good in these old territorial areas, there is a decided trend to take them because of traditional affiliations. I have data on the clan and blood relationships in three of these range assignments and this is reasonably complete only on that from the Bylas district in the Point of Pines and Clover region. What data there is on the former two shows that at least a part of each is made up of close blood and clan relatives. In the White Mountain body 3 clans and three or four distinct families are strongly represented. However, there is considerable relationship between certain of these families, either by blood or by affinity.

Goodwin's report tends to verify Kitch's statement that the Indian cattle industry was organized basically in terms of native socio-political units. He also introduced a point that did not appear elsewhere in the records – that there was a definite trend for range groups to move their cattle onto territory that had formerly been occupied by the principal socio-political unit, or units, making up the new range groups.

In 1936, Morris Opler, Assistant Anthropologist in the Washington office of the Bureau of Indian Affairs, made a brief visit to San Carlos. On the basis of this visit, Opler criticized the San Carlos administration for not paying enough attention to native Indian units or socio-political organization in administering the affairs of the reservation. In reply, Kitch pointed out certain difficulties inherent in attempting to have members of the Tribal Business Committee elected solely in terms of the native socio-political units. He then pointed out that the Indian cattle industry was being organized in terms of family or clan groups.

> As a matter of development, both by clans and by industrial requirements, I believe that Mr. Opler could have found out that in building up our cattle community groups, we have used almost exclusively the clan relationship, thereby mingling business methods or business administration in cattle management with their old clan relationships.
>
> You will note that our grouping of cattle interests is almost entirely based on clan affiliation or relationships. As an example, the San Carlos or river unit, is a group of Indians owning a small group of cattle who desire to have their cattle adjacent to the San Carlos River. The same is true of the Bylas, our second group, they being Coyoteros on the Gila River. Our third group is known as the Victor range, it being composed of Indians of the SI [*sic*] and related bands, of which old Victor Emanuel was the leading spirit. In our next group, we find the Stevens range, which is composed of the Stevens

boys, together with such friends and relatives of the old relationships that existed many years ago. The Cassadore range, our fifth range, is composed of Indians related to band Chief Cassadore and those friendly with that clan. We then have the Circle Seven range, which is composed of Henry Chinn and others who desire to affiliate in a co-operative group due to friends and family ties. We then have the Ash Creek range, which is a community range composed of both Bylas and San Carlos Indians. A Mohave range for Mohaves south of the Coolidge reservoir makes another group. We are developing for the Tonto band the grazing area formerly used by Mrs. Zee Hayes, which is claimed by them to be their early home. The Sago group or clan is located at Point of Pines with another group of related Indians known as the Moses group on a portion of the Double Circle range. I believe this clearly indicates that instead of believing that groups or clans are unimportant that this type of community grouping has been a primary factor in our distribution of ranges.

This statement indicates that by 1936 ten groups, or companies, of cattle-owning Indians had been established, with each group using a particular area of range for its cattle. The following summary shows the term by which each group was designated, the basis for membership in the group, and the range used by each.

The use of the terms "band," "clan," and "group," as a basis for membership in these range groups would seem to indicate that Kitch did try to establish the Indian cattle industry on the basis of native socio-political units. This is one of the principles which students of culture change point out is necessary in successfully carrying out a program of directed culture change.

It would seem, therefore, that in most of the range groups there were nuclei consisting of members of native socio-political units. It is very doubtful that the bands referred to were the pre-reservation socio-political units. Instead, the term band probably refers to the tag bands. The SI band, mentioned as going onto the Victor range, was actually the SE tag band, which did move its cattle onto the Victor range. However, Goodwin has pointed out that "in almost all cases the local

Term for group	*Basis of group membership*	*Range used*
San Carlos	"desire to have their cattle adjacent to the San Carlos River"	San Carlos River range
Bylas	"Coyoteros"	Gila River
Victor	"SI [actually SE tag band] and related bands" headed by Victor Emanuel	Victor
Stevens	"Stevens boys, together with such friends and relatives of the old relationships"	Stevens
Cassadore	"related to band Chief Cassadore, and those friendly with that clan"	Cassadore
Circle Seven	"Henry Chinn and others, . . . in a cooperative group due to friends and family ties"	Circle Seven
Ash Creek	"Community . . . composed of . . . Bylas and San Carlos Indians"	Ash Creek
Mohave	"for Mohaves"	South of Coolidge Reservoir
Tonto	"for the Tonto band"	Zee Hayes
Sago Group	"Sago group or clan . . . with another group of related Indians known as the Moses group"	Portion of Double Circle

groups combined in one tag band came from the same aboriginal band." On the other hand, the use of terms such as "friends," "friendly," and "both Bylas and San Carlos Indians," clearly indicates that there was some amount of heterogeneity involved in the membership of the range groups in 1936. This initial heterogeneity of range-group membership is undoubtedly related directly to the breakdown of the pre-reservation socio-political units and, later, of the tag bands. The factors causing the disintegration of the socio-political units have been described in Chapter 2.

Formation of Cattle Associations

Having described the establishment of the range groups of Indian cattlemen, it is now necessary to outline the transformation of these range groups into formally organized associations.

It has been pointed out that the documentary evidence indicates that there was some heterogeneity in the membership of the range groups as they were established. Kitch stated that the "grouping of cattle interests is almost entirely based on clan affiliation or relationships." This statement is acceptable only if it is considered to refer to a nucleus of related families, but with other, and often unrelated, families and individuals attached to the nuclear group. His further comments refer to people who were "friendly" to the nuclear unit becoming a part of a range group. Goodwin also points out that each of the range groups was "headed by an influential man, the leader of the enterprise."

Interviews with Indian cattlemen during the course of this study emphasized the fact that each range group had a nucleus of related families, but that other unrelated families and individuals were members of each range group from the beginning. The following are representative statements made by some of these Indian cattlemen.

> "The associations were not based on clans or bands when formed. They were mixed from the beginning. Circle Seven was formed of Mohaves, Tontos, San Carlos, and Coyoteros. And they are still mixed. . . . The associations were not formed around one tag-band, they were all mixed."

> "The ranges of the White outfits were occupied by mixed groups of Apaches."

> "When the Double Circle range was taken over, Superintendent Kitch asked, not told, a group of families to run cattle on the Point of Pines range. The Moses, Kindelay, and Pike families moved their stock to the Point of Pines range. The Moses and Kindelay families were related, but neither one was related to the Pike family — just good friends."

> "The associations were mixed from the beginning. There were some family groups, but also others."

> "Kitch was the man who started the Indians in the cattle business in a big way. And Hi Brown was the superintendent of the Livestock Association. We, in the Victor family, formed the Victor Association. We couldn't operate alone, so we formed an association. And other family groups went on other ranges. The Stevenses went around Slaughter Mountain; the Polks over on Circle Seven; Moses and Sago families to Clover; and Pike and Kindelay to the area around BS Gap. . . . But up at Hilltop that was mixed. . . . And at Ash Creek, I don't know, lots of people went there."

The file records of families forming the associations in late 1939 tend to verify the above statements by Indian informants. There seem to have been certain families serving as nuclei for each association group, with other families filling out the association membership.

During this study it was assumed that those Indians whose socio-political groups had occupied a particular portion of the reservation area in pre-reservation times would join the association, or associations, using range land in that area.

In order to test the validity of this assumption, pertinent data regarding the relationships between the bands and the associations were brought together, as shown in Table 1. Band membership was traced through tag-band affiliation, a step not shown here. It should be emphasized that the associations listed in this table are those that were in operation in the latter half of 1939. The reader will note the difference between these associations and those listed for May, 1938, or for January, 1941.

Analysis of Table 1, in terms of pre-reservation bands and the late 1939 associations, shows that most of the members of the Apache Peaks

TABLE 1
Association Membership by Band, 1939

	Ash Creek	*Bylas*	*Slaughter Mountain*	*Clover*	*Point of Pines*	*Victor*	*Cassadore*	*Circle Seven*	*Tin Cup*	*Tonto*	*Mohave*
Apache Peaks	4	—	—	—	1	3	2	25	4	1	1
Aravaipa	18	10	1	1	8	11	2	1	10	1	2
Pinal	20	2	1	2	11	—	7	19	18	1	2
San Carlos	4	4	2	—	3	—	20	9	3	—	—
San Carlos Group Total	46	16	4	3	23	14	31	54	35	3	5
E. White Mt.	19	9	11	22	11	—	—	—	—	—	—
W. White Mt.	9	8	4	8	13	—	—	—	—	—	1
White Mt. Total	28	17	15	30	24	—	—	—	—	—	1
So. Tonto	8	4	8	4	25	1	7	12	14	6	—
So. & No. Tonto	7	1	—	—	2	—	—	3	5	7	1
Mohave	—	—	1	—	—	—	1	1	—	4	14

band entered the Circle Seven Association. People of the Aravaipa band went mainly into the Ash Creek Association, but they also entered two other associations on the west side of the reservation area – Victor and Tin Cup, as well as the more southerly Bylas Association. The Pinal people entered, in nearly equal numbers, the Ash Creek, Circle Seven, and Tin Cup associations. Members of the San Carlos band entered primarily the Cassadore Association. These four bands form Goodwin's "San Carlos Group." Looking at the group as a whole, it is evident that some of the people were attracted by the good forage on the Ash Creek and Point of Pines ranges. However, most of them entered associations in the western part of the reservation. This was the part of the reservation area that was occupied by these bands in pre-reservation times.

The "White Mountain Group" consisted of two bands. When these people were given the opportunity to return to the White Mountain area, some of them chose to remain on the San Carlos Reservation. Table 1 shows very clearly that members of these two bands entered principally the Clover, Ash Creek, and Point of Pines associations, and to a lesser extent the Bylas and Slaughter Mountain associations. The Clover, Point of Pines, and Slaughter Mountain ranges are in the eastern part of the reservation, which is the area occupied by these White Mountain bands in pre-reservation times. These people, also, were attracted by the good forage on the Ash Creek range, and they lived at Bylas.

The designation "Southern Tonto" refers to three tag bands which Goodwin says were entirely Southern Tonto. They went overwhelmingly to the good range of the Point of Pines Association. Otherwise, they were most strongly attracted to the two associations in the western part of the reservation – Tin Cup and Circle Seven. Their pre-reservation area was west of the reservation.

The term "Southern and Northern Tonto" refers to five tag bands which Goodwin says combined people from both groups of Tontos. Aside from their attraction to the Ash Creek range, these people went mainly into two associations in the western part of the reservation, Tonto and Tin Cup.

Most of the Mohave people formed an association of the same name in the southwestern part of the reservation. A few went into the Tonto Association, also in the southwestern part of the reservation.

It should be noted that in pre-reservation

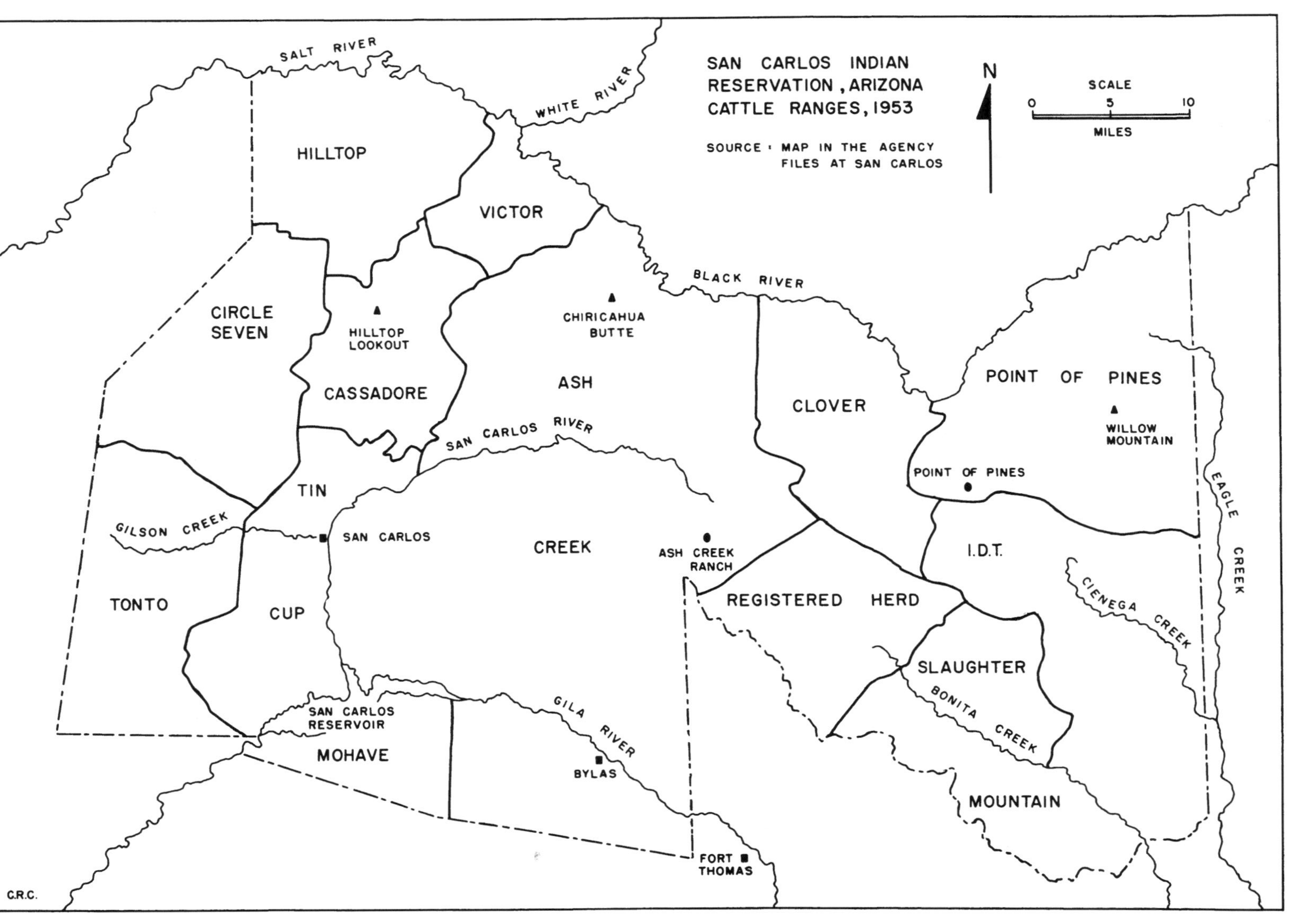
SAN CARLOS INDIAN
RESERVATION, ARIZONA
CATTLE RANGES, 1953
SOURCE: MAP IN THE AGENCY
FILES AT SAN CARLOS
N
SCALE
0 5 10
MILES
EAGLE CREEK
POINT OF PINES
WILLOW MOUNTAIN
Point of Pines
CIENEGA CREEK
I.D.T.
SLAUGHTER
BONITA CREEK
MOUNTAIN
CLOVER
REGISTERED HERD
BLACK RIVER
ASH CREEK RANCH
FORT THOMAS
WHITE RIVER
CHIRICAHUA BUTTE
ASH
SAN CARLOS RIVER
CREEK
GILA RIVER
BYLAS
VICTOR
SALT RIVER
HILLTOP
HILLTOP LOOKOUT
CASSADORE
SAN CARLOS
SAN CARLOS RESERVOIR
MOHAVE
TIN
CUP
CIRCLE SEVEN
GILSON CREEK
TONTO
C.R.C.

times neither the Mohaves (Yavapais) nor Tontos occupied any part of the area now included in the reservation. Otherwise, the evidence proves the assumption that Indians joining associations went into those organizations whose ranges lay in areas occupied by their bands in pre-reservation times.

Since Superintendent Kitch emphasized that the associations were "almost entirely based on clan affiliation or relationships," it would be very helpful to be able to outline the relationships between clans and associations. This is not possible because of the lack of information about the clan affiliations of the members of the 1939 associations.

In a letter dated April 12, 1937, Kitch reported:

> I feel that our movement in the grouping of clan groups of individual owners is well on its way but this completed or organized work must progress slowly. We now have them organized but without charter papers signed excepting a few cases, but by next fall hope to have all of our groups signed up in regular organized community groups.

In another letter written June 8, 1937, Kitch made the following statement regarding the Indian-occupied ranges:

> You will note this includes ten separate sales covering six of our range districts, Gila River being shown as both Mohave and Bylas districts, both in the Gila River area. Our remaining districts were not worked for spring sales as their feed is particularly adapted to fall sales. This includes the Tribal range, Sago range, Moses range, the Double Circle range, and the Stevens range.

In the file entitled, "Stock Raising, Cattle Associations, General," Folder No. 1 covers the period from February 1, 1932, to June 30, 1938. In this folder, but bearing no date, is a blank mimeographed copy of "Articles of Association and By-Laws of Livestock Association." Attached to this and also bearing no dates, are sheets showing the names of Indian cattle owners – and their brands – who were running cattle on the following ranges. These are listed here in the same order as in the file, with the number of individuals using each range.

Gila River	41	F	19
San Carlos	58	Cassadore	35
Eagle Creek	46	Circle Seven	64
Ash Creek	96	Sago	35
Robert Roy	23	Moses	24
Tin Cup	16	Stevens	41
Victor	11	Total	509

On June 22, 1938, the San Carlos Tribal Council recognized and officially sanctioned the existence of the reservation cattle associations by means of the following ordinance:

> Relating to the establishment of voluntary cattle associations upon the San Carlos Indian Reservation, Arizona.
>
> Be it enacted by the San Carlos Tribal Council in special meeting on June 22, 1938.
>
> Section 1. That the following ten Cattle Associations together with their Articles of Incorporation and By-laws, copies of which are herewith submitted, be approved:
>
> Apache Mohave Livestock Association
> Tonto Livestock Association
> Cassadore Livestock Association
> Victor SE Livestock Association
> Clover Livestock Association
> Ash Creek Livestock Association
> Slaughter Mountain Livestock Association
> Circle Seven Livestock Association
> Point of Pines Cattle Association
>
> The foregoing Ordinance was, on June 22, 1938, duly adopted by a vote of 6 for and 0 against, by the San Carlos Tribal Council, pursuant to authority vested in it by Section 8, Article V, of the Constitution of the Tribe, ratified by the Tribe on October 19, 1935, pursuant to Section 16 of the Act of June 18, 1934, (48 Stat. 984). Said ordinance is effective as of the date of its approval by the Superintendent of the San Carlos Indian Reservation, subject to its rescission by the Secretary of the Interior pursuant to Section 17, Article V, of the Constitution and by-laws of the San Carlos Apache Tribe. Approved 6-29-38, by Lewis F. Brown, Senior Clerk in Charge.

It should be noted that while the wording of the ordinance refers to "ten Cattle Associations," only nine are listed.

The last item in this folder is an undated list of the livestock associations, showing the date on which each association adopted its by-laws and articles of incorporation, together with the number of individual owners signing each document.

Date	*Association*	*Number of owners signing:* *By-Laws*	*Art. of Inc.*
2-20-37	Victor (SE)	11	11
9- 8-37	Clover	28	24
9-16-37	Ash Creek	44	53
9-21-37	Slaughter Mt.	20	20
9-22-37	Mohave Apache	12	12
10- 7-37	Circle Seven	40	22
10-11-37	Cassadore	32	18
3-18-38	Tonto	15	15
5- 3-38	Point of Pines	18	36

This list is the same as that given in the ordinance of June 22, 1938, however it should be noted that in some instances there are discrepancies between the number of individuals signing the by-laws and the number signing the articles of incorporation. It is not clear why there should be this discrepancy, and it was not explained in the materials in the file.

In the offices at San Carlos there is a series of files covering the individual cattle associations. Some of these files include the date of formation of the association. Where these dates are given they are the same as those shown above.

In addition to the nine associations listed above with the dates of their formal organization, there are two others to be accounted for. A letter dated October 18, 1939, from one regional official of the Bureau of Indian Affairs to another, states that

> there are two other groups, Hill Top and Tin Cup, functioning similar to the above associations. These two groups are now in the process of developing their Articles of Association and By-Laws.

The next listing of the cattle associations is in Folder No. 3 of the same file. This folder contains several items concerning a joint meeting of the San Carlos Tribal Council and directors of 11 cattle growers' associations on January 13, 1941. These associations were:

Ash Creek	Mohave
Bylas	Point of Pines
Clover	Tin Cup
Circle Seven	Tonto
Cassadore	Victor
Hilltop	

Comparing this 1941 list of associations with those established by the ordinance of June 22, 1938, it will be noted that there are three new associations: Bylas, Hilltop, and Tin Cup. On the other hand, the Slaughter Mountain Association which was included in the ordinance is not listed in the minutes of the joint meeting in 1941. It is possible that this was an oversight in the minutes, or that this association was not represented by any of its directors at this meeting. Whatever the reason may be, the Slaughter Mountain Association was included in the 1938 ordinance, and is included in a list of associations for 1942.

The list of January 22, 1942, shows 12 associations, but goes on immediately to say that "Bylas has already combined with Ash Creek."

Three lists for the year 1944 show the following associations:

Ash Creek	Point of Pines
Cassadore	Slaughter Mountain
Circle Seven	Tin Cup
Clover	Tonto
Hilltop	Victor
Mohave	

The only variation in these three lists is that one shows a Willow Mountain Association instead of Point of Pines. However, the two names refer to the same association, Willow Mountain being a prominent landmark in the Point of Pines area.

A list for 1953 shows the same associations as for 1944, and these same associations were operating at the conclusion of the field research for this study in 1955. However, in 1956 a reorganization of the San Carlos Indian cattle industry was begun, one result of which was a decrease in the number of associations. This reorganization is described in Chapter 7.

Relation of Associations to Ranges

The range areas occupied by the various associations were very unequal in size. During this study, Indian cattlemen were asked why and how this happened. The following statements are representative of the replies:

> "Because the Indians all had their cattle on Ash Flat, and they got to be too many, so they split up. Some went to Clover, some to Point of Pines, some to Hilltop. But most of them stayed on Ash Flat."

TABLE 2
Ranges on San Carlos Reservation

Designation of Range	*Last Permittee and Final Year*		*Name of Indian Range*	*1955 Association Using Range*
A	Mrs. Blake Hayes	1936	-F-	Tonto
B	Hayes Livestock Co.	1938	-F-	Tonto
C	San Pasqual Cattle Co.	1934	Circle Seven	Circle Seven
D	John Osborne	1934	IDA	Hilltop
E	G. A. Bryce	1934	Stevens	Slaughter Mountain
F	Double Circle	1937		
	Lee Bros.	1938	Eagle Creek	IDT and Slaughter Mountain
G	Double Circle	1937	Eagle Creek	Point of Pines
H	Chiricahua Cattle Co.	1930	Victor	Victor
I	Chiricahua Cattle Co.	1914	Indian	Cassadore
J	Chiricahua Cattle Co.	1930	Ash Creek	Ash Creek
K	None		San Carlos	Tin Cup
L	None		Gila River	Ash Creek
M	Chiricahua Cattle Co.	1927	Ash Flat	Registered Herd
N	Double Circle	1937	Sago	Clover
O	None		Robert Roy	Mohave
P	Double Circle ?	1937?	?	Point of Pines

"I think it is because some of the White men who ran cattle on the reservation had big ranges and some had small. Like the Chiricahua Cattle Company, it had most of the range that the Ash Creek has now. Some of the others had smaller ranges on the reservation, and they had other ranges by the reservation."

"The Ash Creek Association range is so big because that's the range that the Chiricahua Cattle Company had. They had some of the Victor range on Blue River too. They had a lot of range. Then up beyond them were the Double Circle. And the Bryce range was where Slaughter Mountain is now. Zee Hayes had part of the Tonto Association range. The Cross-S and Wineglass were in the western area too . . . in the Circle Seven area."

"I don't know for sure why the cattle associations vary so much in size. The Double Circle took in the area now in the Point of Pines Association. And the CCC was up on Ash Flat. But I don't know about the others."

These informants and other Indian cattlemen generally agreed that the size of an association range depended upon the area occupied by the White permittee who was replaced by a group of Indians. Proof of this opinion may be seen in Table 2, which shows the relationships between the former lettered ranges, the last White permittees who occupied them and the final year of such occupation, the designations of the ranges as the Indians occupied them, and the name of the association using the various ranges.

Several factors determined the amount of range that was occupied by each White permittee. Among these factors were size, strength, and location of the permittee's off-reservation operation, and the nature of the topography on the adjacent portion of the reservation.

Changes in Associations

Changes in associations, prior to 1956, took place in regard to name, area, membership, and number.

The following list gives the changes that occurred in the names of some of the associations.

Name, 1953	*Former Name*
Ash Creek (Bylas)	Ash Flat (Gila River Cattle Association)
Cassadore	–
Circle Seven	Seven Mile
Clover	–
Hilltop	Sawmill
Mohave	–
Point of Pines	Willow Mountain
Slaughter Mountain	–
Tin Cup	San Carlos
Tonto	? -F-
Victor	–
Registered Herd	Ash Flat
IDT	East End

The times when these changes occurred, and the reasons for them, could not be ascertained during this study.

Except when associations merged, as when Bylas merged with Ash Creek in 1942, their range areas have remained essentially constant since their establishment. Disputes regarding the location of boundaries between associations apparently required only an agreement as to what constituted the boundary line. This did not necessarily involve the actual transfer of land. It was more a matter of eliminating uncertainty.

Several informants stated that Indian cattlemen did not necessarily remain in the association which they first entered. In order to check these statements a list was made which showed in one column the names of all members of the range groups as they existed in 1937–38, in a second column the name of the association which each person entered at that time, and in a third column the name of the association of which each survivor was a member in 1953. The number of entries in the third column is relatively small, since many of the founding members of the associations were no longer alive in 1953. The aim of this analysis was to determine how many of the original association members who were still alive in 1953 had remained in the one association, and how many had transferred to another association. A summary of this analysis is shown in Table 3.

A quick glance shows that a majority of the cattlemen remained in the association which they first entered, as is shown by the large numbers running diagonally from left to right in the table. The only significant case of change from one association to another is that of Point of Pines

TABLE 3
Interassociation Transfers, 1937-1953

From: / *To:*	*Ash Creek*	*Bylas*	*Cassadore*	*Circle Seven*	*Clover*	*Hilltop*	*Mohave*	*Point of Pines*	*Slaughter Mountain*	*Tin Cup*	*Tonto*	*Victor*
Ash Creek	38	—	—	1	1	1	—	—	1	—	—	—
Bylas	5	—	1	—	—	—	—	2	—	—	—	—
Cassadore	—	—	24	1	—	—	—	—	—	—	—	—
Circle Seven	—	—	—	30	1	—	—	1	—	—	4	—
Clover	—	—	—	—	24	—	—	—	—	—	—	—
Hilltop	1	—	—	—	—	18	—	—	—	—	—	—
Mohave	3	—	2	—	—	—	8	—	—	2	—	—
Point of Pines	2	—	—	—	2	16	1	20	1	1	1	—
Slaughter Mt.	—	—	—	—	—	—	1	1	23	—	—	—
Tin Cup	5	—	—	4	—	1	—	—	—	5	—	—
Tonto	2	—	—	—	—	—	2	—	—	—	12	—
Victor	—	—	3	—	—	—	—	—	—	—	—	5

people transferring to Hilltop. The reasons for this change could not be determined at the time of this study. Clover Association shows no changes. This may be due to the fact that Clover, with its high elevation, probably had better forage. Referring again to Point of Pines, its forage was equally as good as Clover, and as good or better than the forage on the Hilltop range. However, the Point of Pines area is the most remote from the centers of population on the reservation, much more so than Hilltop. This may have been a factor in the transfer from Point of Pines to Hilltop. Most of the other associations show very few transfers.

Probably one important factor in the stability of association membership is that the Indian cattleman initially made an effort to get into the association where he had friends and relatives. Therefore, he was likely to stay in that association. That there were transfers is due in part to the fact that a person could not always enter immediately the association of his choice (this will be explained in Chapter 5) and thus would transfer to the desired association as soon as possible. Transfers might also be due to friction with other members, or because range resources might be better in another association area.

Tribal Herds

In addition to cattle operations on the basis of individual ownership, such operations were carried on (1) by the Bureau of Indian Affairs for the benefit of the tribe as a whole, and (2), more recently, by the Tribal Council acting for the entire tribe. There was not sufficient documentation available to make possible a presentation here of the full history of the tribal herds. The information that was available is presented in the following brief historical statement.

The earliest specific statement in reference to a tribal herd which could be found in the files was dated April 4, 1919. This concerned a charge of $10,000 against this herd for stock purchased for it. However, a report on the tribal herd as of November 1, 1921, includes a financial statement of the cost of the herd from June, 1914, to June 30, 1921. This would seem to indicate that the tribal herd, referred to by the Brand IDA – Indian Department Agency – had been first established in 1914. It is also a matter of record that Range I (more recently Cassadore Association range) was withdrawn from permit in 1914 for use by the tribal herd. Some further evidence concerning the year 1914 as a beginning date is contained in the Soil Conservation Service report (1938:2) which states that "since 1914 there had been a small tribal herd maintained by the Agency."

In addition to the IDA there was also an IDS herd – Indian Department School – which was maintained for the benefit of the boarding school at Rice. This distinction in herds was abandoned about 1925. In a letter dated March 26, 1925, to Kitch, Commissioner Merritt suggested

> that certain animals which are now being run with the IDS brand, the descendants of the former beef herd at the Rice Indian School, be consolidated with the main tribal herd which is branded IDA. Since these IDS cattle are being run with the other herd and cared for by agency employees, it is felt that all of the cattle being run as ID stock should be branded with the IDA or agency brand.

Under the date of September 19, 1919, there were in the files at San Carlos at the time of this study 21 certificates of entry in the American Hereford Record for that number of Hereford bulls. The breeder was William E. Wallace of Midland, Texas. These bulls were placed with the tribal herd.

In the files there were also circulars, dated February, 1920, advertising 240 head of Indian cattle and 940 head of IDA (tribal herd) cattle for sale.

In the file entitled "Stock Raising – Tribal Herd," there were counts of the number of head of cattle in the tribal herd for a few years. In 1920 – 6053; 1921 – 4100; 1922 – 3996; 1923 – 3326.

In March, 1926, Kitch wrote to the commissioner: "It is our program to purchase sixty additional pure bred bulls this year and place them in the tribal herd. This will permit us to take a number of the tribal herd bulls and place them with the Indian cattle on Ash Flat. . . ."

In July, 1927, Kitch mentioned four roundup wagons in operation, one of which was the IDA or tribal wagon.

The Soil Conservation Report (1938:2) states that "the tribal herd of 2,000, approximately 1,000 of which are registered Herefords, remains as sort of a nursery, breeding fine cattle which are issued to individual Indians at cost."

Registered Herd

As early as 1933 action was initiated to make the tribal herd a registered herd. On April 27 of that year the Tribal Business Committee recommended officially:

> That authority be granted and funds appropriated for the purchase of registered Hereford heifers by which a registered herd for purpose of breeding bulls for individual Indians can be established on the present tribal range, gradually replacing the present herd of grade cattle in accordance with recommendations of Superintendent Kitch under date of January 17, 1933, file Ext. 1313-33.

The action recommended here became a reality the following year. Superintendent McCray wrote in the *American Cattle Producer* (1941:2):

> During 1934 the government purchased a large number of cattle from drought areas. From these, this reservation was furnished 600 registered Hereford heifers on a replacement plan. These were placed on the tribal herd range. The tribe purchased about 30 registered bulls from the Colorado Painter herd to run with these heifers. From this breeding, some fine, purebred cattle were produced. It was not possible, however, to register these cattle. A plan had to be devised to control and record the breeding so registration would be possible.

Apparently, it was not until 1938 that steps were taken to control the purebred herd so that it could become a registered herd. Superintendent McCray, writing in 1943 in reply to an inquiry, stated:

> In the spring of 1938 this Agency purchased Painter's Domino Number C366 with two of his calves (male), Painter's Domino 219 and Painter's Domino 185. During the fall and winter of 1938 all registered cows as well as the best of the purebred heifers and cows were moved to Ash Flat. During the spring of 1939 corrals and other facilities for breeding by Artificial Insemination were built. We also built a small field laboratory. Mr. John T. Montgomery, then Regional Director of Extension in this area, secured for us the services of a young technician, John F. Lasley, from the University of Missouri. For the past four breeding seasons Mr. Lasley has conducted this breeding program, using Painter's Domino 366 as much as possible. Number 219 has developed into an excellent bull and results from his breeding are quite as satisfactory as that from 366. The purpose of this project is to produce superior range bulls for exclusive use on the reservation.

In a booklet, *San Carlos Hereford Feeder Sales,* there is a further statement concerning the artificial insemination program.

> This method of breeding is still being used and enabled Painter's Domino C. 366th to sire over 2500 calves while he was on the reservation. In 1945, WHR Royalmix was purchased from the Wyoming Hereford Ranch to replace the 366th. In 1947 another bull, WHR Invader 14th, was purchased from the same ranch to supplement Royalmix. The use of these fine Hereford bulls has been of great help in improving the quality of the San Carlos cattle.

The registered herd was still operating full scale at the time this report was being written. Through the years of its existence it has furnished bulls for the association ranges. From this herd many Apaches, starting in the cattle business, have drawn 20 or 30 head of heifers. The registered herd has also provided cattle for the other tribal herd, the IDT. The program of artificial insemination was discontinued after 1955.

IDT or Social Security Herd

A resolution passed by the San Carlos Tribal Council on December 6, 1938, established a second tribal herd, distinct from the registered herd:

> Whereas there are a number of old people, widows, orphans and others living on the San Carlos Indian Reservation who are unable, by their own efforts, to make a living from the reservation and have no other means of support; and
>
> Whereas this body wishes to insure all helpless members of the tribe their rightful share of the reservation income;
>
> Be it Therefore Resolved that there shall be developed, on the East side of the San Carlos Indian Reservation, a tribal pure-bred herd of Hereford cattle; that this herd shall be built up to and maintained at approximately 5,000 head;

that it shall be under Agency management; that surplus heifers from this herd shall be available for reimbursable sale to San Carlos Indians without cattle, and others; and that after running expenses are deducted, such of the profits as are necessary shall be used for the support of all Indians without support (San Carlos Apaches) 65 years and older, helpless widows, orphan children, and others, i.e., blind, cripples, etc.

Superintendent McCray, in his article in the *American Cattle Producer* (1941:7), discussed further the social problem that caused the IDT herd to be established.

> The reservation and its resources are tribal community property. A planned economy that left out the support of these helpless people would be unfair and incomplete. A system of taxation of productive Indians was considered and rejected. The council finally agreed that a better plan would be to set aside a range on the east side of the reservation, stock it, and use the proceeds for those requiring relief. . . . The council authorized the use of $75,000 of tribal funds for the purchase of a foundation herd, and the social security herd came into being. The herd now consists of over 3,000 head of cows and heifers. . . .The proceeds from sales are placed in two accounts: one to cover operating costs, and the other for social security payments.

An additional statement regarding the establishment and successful operation of the IDT herd is in the 1948 booklet previously referred to:

> Surplus cows from the registered herd together with select young cows from individual Indian grade herds were used as a foundation stock. Only select bulls were sent to this range for breeding purposes. As a result the steers from this herd carrying the IDT brand have won the reputation of being some of the best steers on the reservation and in the state of Arizona.

One Indian informant stated that the old IDA (agency) brand was changed to IDT (tribal) when the associations were being formed in 1937–38. A search was made in the available files to verify this statement, but without success.

An officer of the Tribal Council stated in an interview in the summer of 1954 that the profits from the operation of the IDT herd had been used for the benefit of Indian indigents on the reservation, but that when the state of Arizona took over the matter of relief these IDT profits were transferred to the support of law and order on the reservation, and for other financial needs of the Tribal Council.

Sales, such as this one at Calva, are conducted by the tribe.

5 OPERATING PROCEDURES

This chapter outlines the operating procedures of the Indian cattle industry on the San Carlos Reservation as of 1955 – the time field work for this study was concluded. No attempt is made to present here all the details of these operations. Such fine details are unnecessary for the purpose of this study, which is to provide a comprehensive report on the origin and development of the cattle industry on this reservation. Furthermore, through the years the details of the operating procedures have undergone many changes, making it practically impossible to give a concise picture of them.

In 1955 there were 11 associations composed of individuals owning cattle. These associations were: Ash Creek, Cassadore, Circle Seven, Clover, Hilltop, Mohave, Point of Pines, Slaughter Mountain, Tin Cup, Tonto, and Victor. Each association had an area of the reservation fenced off for its range. In addition there were separate ranges for the two tribal herds, the registered and the IDT.

Personnel

Extension Agent

The extension agent was the general supervisor of the Indian cattle industry. All major decisions and, undoubtedly, many minor ones, concerning the activities of the cattle associations were made by him. All of the accounts and budgets of the cattle industry, including those of the associations, were handled by the extension agent and his staff. As is discussed in more detail in a later chapter, it is this author's opinion that these procedures continued the paternalistic activities of the Bureau of Indian Affairs, simply shifting the responsibility in this case from the superintendent to the extension agent.

Line Riders

These men patrolled the reservation boundaries on horseback, with each rider assigned a specific section of line. Each made any fence repairs he could, and reported major damages. It was his duty to check for trespassers. He noted the condition of forage, water, and salt in range areas adjacent to the boundary. He could move cattle to better forage or water, and he treated diseased or injured livestock to the best of his ability.

Since line riders were paid by the tribal government, the Tribal Council had to approve each man hired for this job. For a period of time there was a supervisor of line riders.

Stockmen

While the extension agent necessarily had to spend much of his time in his office at San Carlos, the stockmen spent their time on the association ranges. The number of stockmen employed fluctuated through the years. In the summer of 1954 only two associations – Ash Creek and Slaughter Mountain – had their own stockmen. Each of the following pairs of associations shared the services of one stockman: Cassadore and Circle Seven, Clover and Point of Pines, Hilltop and Victor, and Tonto and Tin Cup. Apparently the stockman for Tonto and Tin Cup provided some service for the Mohave Association. Ash Creek was the only association to have an Anglo as a stockman. All the other stockmen were Apaches.

One of the tribal herds, the IDT, had a stockman in charge. There was a foreman for the registered-herd range whose duties were essentially the same as those of a stockman.

In the normal course of his duties the stockman would supervise, or perform, the following activities:

(1) Overseeing work of the line riders and other range hands.
(2) Branding, castrating, and dehorning cattle.
(3) Checking the animals for disease and injury.
(4) Shifting cattle to make the best use of forage and water.
(5) Checking placement of salt.
(6) Checking ratio of bulls to cows.
(7) Checking fences, traps, corrals, and chutes.
(8) Cutting out cattle for sales.
(9) Driving the cattle to the sale pens at Calva or San Carlos.
(10) Checking the status of association funds and budgets.
(11) Acting as an adviser to, and executive for, the association board of directors.

The stockmen and line riders were paid by the tribal government from a fund composed of fees paid by individual owners at sale time.

Other Range Personnel

Each association was supposed to hire range hands who carried out many of the duties listed for the stockman and line riders. In the summer of 1954, Cassadore, Circle Seven, Mohave, Tin Cup, and Victor associations did not have any full-time range hands. With the other associations the number of range hands varied from one on up, and from part time to full time.

Care of the Cattle

An important consideration in the care of the cattle on the reservation is the moving of the stock periodically in order to insure a sufficient amount of forage and water. If there are no fences to block them the cattle will drift from one area to another, and north and south seasonally. This is where the human element is important – to see that the right gates are open at the right time. The human element is also very important in the proper handling of traps, so that the animals are not confined too long. Loss of stock can result from improper work by the range personnel. At the higher altitudes it is necessary to keep the block salt free of snow cover.

It is imperative that the bulls be well distributed over each association range. It may be necessary to move some of them, in order to keep a good cow-bull ratio, and thus have more assurance of a good calf crop.

One of the most frequent complaints voiced by BIA personnel and by many of the Indians is that the range personnel are too much inclined to run the cattle. As one Indian informant put it: "These Indian cowboys run cattle too much. They holler at 'em and race 'em. It makes 'em wild." If a calf has a wild mother, it is more than likely that the calf also will be wild. This can cause a loss of stock at roundup when it may be impossible to get some of the wild stock out of brushy, rocky country.

Roundup

In a majority of years most of the associations had two roundups each year, fall and spring. Because of poor range conditions some associations were able to have only one roundup a year, usually in the fall.

At roundup time each individual cattle owner was expected to participate or furnish a man to take his place. In this regard, a resolution dated September 4, 1945, said in part:

> Owners of cattle must report on roundups or furnish a man in their place. The practice of collecting a branding fee from owners not represented is resulting in many taking this way to get their work done. It is impossible to get adequate help unless cattle owners get out and do their share of the work.

Each owner who failed to participate in the roundup or send a substitute was subject to a penalty of $5.00 per calf branded in his brand. The difficulties the association encountered in getting owners to do their part in the roundups were reflected in a statement made by a BIA field official that "some of them [associations] must hire help to work the cattle, which is an unnecessary cost, which should be saved by each man doing his share of the work."

In the case of owners who had steady jobs, a few took time off to participate in the roundups. Most of the employed owners sent men to work in their places. For those owners who did participate, the length of time they had to work varied with the associations. In all associations, at the time of this study, the number of owners who participated in the roundup was very inadequate, so that it was necessary to hire range hands for the occasion. For the fall roundup of one of the smaller associations in 1954 only four owners showed up.

All of the associations had some amount of very rough and brushy range. It was very difficult for experienced cowboys to get the cattle out of such country. Such experienced men complained bitterly that the hired range hands did not even attempt to get the cattle that took off into rough country. Such conditions increased the number of mavericks and other wild cattle. One experienced cattle owner said: "Fellows working on roundups don't know the country, can't get the cattle out. They even get lost themselves."

The two most serious problems in connection with the roundups were lack of men, and the apparent lack of sufficient horses. Superintendent McCray (1941:7) called attention to the spread of the dourine disease among the horses on the reservation in the 1930's, and the necessary slaughter of large numbers of the animals. He said that

> the reservation was almost entirely free from horses when the work was completed. Horses are necessary to cattle work. The tribe decided to raise their own cow-horses. They purchased some good mares and three good stallions. They set aside a horse range. This has been operating nearly five years and is producing some fine cow-horses.

At the time of this study, there was considerable difference of opinion as to whether or not there were sufficient horses on the reservation for roundup purposes. Most of the Indians maintained that there were not enough, while some Indians and most of the bureau personnel felt that there were. One bureau official said that there were enough horses but that the Indians did not want to use them. On the other hand, one of the association stockmen in the summer of 1954 said that he had just come back from a trip off-reservation looking for horses to buy for his association. It was his firm opinion that the tribe should have kept the horse range referred to in Superintendent McCray's comments, and which had been abolished. The keeping of the horses has apparently been a problem back through the years. Should all horses be kept on a central range, or should each association have its own range or pasture for horses? Should horses be owned by individual stockmen, or by the associations, or by the tribe?

In a meeting of the Tribal Council in December, 1950, several statements were made regarding the problem of keeping horses.

> . . . every member belonging to various associations is supposed to keep his horses in his own association or is entitled to keep two horses if he feeds them and keeps them in pens.
>
> . . . some associations have private horse pastures within their own association. . . .
>
> . . . some people are not members of associations but still they own some horses and do not have any cattle or range assigned to them.
>
> . . . it was suggested that land north and across the river from the residence district be set aside and it was agreed to do this, and the president of the Ash Creek Association said they would allow this land to be used as a [horse] pasture for the people who have no cattle. However the title of this land will remain in the Ash Creek Cattle Association and permission must be obtained from the Ash Creek Association before placing horses in this pasture.

One young Apache cattle owner said that more fellows in his association would go out on roundup but "they don't have horses." He said that when he started in the cattle business he had four horses, but that as a result of lending them to other fellows he was down to one in 1954. Another young cattle owner, who was taking one month off from his regular job to work in the 1954 fall roundup of his association, said that there were not enough horses to work the roundup as it should be. He said that his association had a few horses, and two or three individuals had some, but that there still were not enough.

There was also a real question as to how many of the available horses were good enough stock and had sufficient training to be efficient in roundup work.

One of the activities in connection with roundup was the cutting out of the cattle to be sold.

The various categories of animals which were cut out for sale purposes are mentioned in the section on sale procedures.

From all association ranges the sale cattle were driven along trails to the sale pens at Calva or San Carlos, whichever was closer. This meant that the cattle from the more distant ranges had to cover long distances on the hoof. Even if conditions along the trail were optimum, the cattle would lose some weight before they reached the sale pen. If water and forage were scarce along the trail, the cattle had to be driven faster, causing a considerable reduction in weight. The matter of weight loss was very important, because the bids at the sale pens, for all classes of cattle but one, were on a per-pound basis.

Branding

On most of the association ranges branding was done only at roundup, which, on the majority of the ranges, meant semi-annually. On the Ash Creek range, branding was done throughout the year by small crews. At roundup, the tally men reported to the roundup foreman or the stockman the number of calves branded in each brand. At sale time all brands were inspected by the Brand Committee, which consisted of three inspectors appointed by the tribal government and paid for the number of days they worked. In case of dispute regarding the brand on an animal, those involved were required to appear before the committee and show proof of their claims. The Brand Committee had to approve new brands, and any changes in brands.

At roundup all mavericks that were caught were given the association brand, and the proceeds from their sale were applied on the operating expenses of the association. From time to time pressure was applied by individual owners to permit such owners to brand any mavericks they found, however the Tribal Council stood firm on this matter.

Until 1954 all cattle on the San Carlos Reservation bore the brand "ID" on the right hip. All other brands – individual, association, or tribal – appeared elsewhere on the animal. The Brand Committee designated the place on the animal where the individual owner's brand was to be placed.

Cattle Sales

Superintendent McCray, in his article in the *American Cattle Producer* (1941:6), summed up very well the history of the sale of Indian-owned cattle on the San Carlos Reservation.

> For a number of years cattle not butchered for home consumption were sold to Indian traders or to the government for use at the school and hospital and for issue to old Indians. As the cattle business grew, this market became inadequate. Local buyers came in and bought the surplus. By 1932 the number of young cattle for sale reached such proportions that the superintendent decided to advertise the sale and interest more buyers. This method brought desirable results. The first annual sale netted approximately $12,000. As Indian-owned cattle spread over the reservation it became necessary to hold several sales. The cattle were gathered at specified places on the reservation and cut into classes. Buyers inspected the cattle, wrote their bid per head on a piece of paper, signed it, and sealed it in an envelope. When they were all in, the bids were opened and sale made to the highest acceptable bidder.
>
> In 1939 the procedure was changed. All salable cattle are now driven to the Southern Pacific Railroad which runs through the reservation. They are graded, classed, and placed in pens. As scales are available, all sales are by the pound. Public auction has replaced sealed bids.

Another means of disposing of the surplus Indian-owned cattle, which was used for some period of time, was by consignment. In a file entitled, "Stock-raising – Cattle Associations – Ash Creek" there is a resolution dated November 9, 1937, signed by the members of the board of directors to consign four carloads of cattle to "a Commission Company for sale on the Los Angeles market."

A resolution by the Tribal Council dated September 3, 1946, states:

> Whereas, the San Carlos Apache Tribe is getting ready for Fall cattle sales, and
>
> Whereas, it has been decided to advertise these cattle sales in a manner so that as many people as possible may be informed
>
> Be it therefore resolved that a half page of advertisement of the San Carlos Cattle Sales be inserted in the weekly Western Livestock Journal.

The amount of this advertisement is to be expended from the fund "S-100, San Carlos Community Fund."

The sales procedures in effect at the time of this study are summarized here.

In the fall of 1956 sales were held on five successive Wednesdays, beginning at 9 a.m. and starting with the first Wednesday in November. Three of the sales were held at Calva and two at San Carlos.

The classes of sale cattle were generally yearling steers, yearling heifers, big steers, cows, mother cows and their calves, stags, and bulls.

All classes of cattle, except cows and calves, were sold by the pound, with the weight determined by scales maintained at the sale pens. Cows and calves were sold as pairs without any weight consideration.

Buyers sat on top of the fence surrounding the sale pen and indicated their bids to the auctioneer by a variety of signals – raising a finger or hand, waving the sale tabulation sheet, nodding the head. The auctioneer was located on an elevated platform in one corner of the sale pen, and operated with a microphone and loudspeaker. At the time of this study, and for many years previously, the auctioneer was Gunter Prude.

One of the stipulations regarding cattle sold was that they must be moved at least 100 miles from the reservation boundary. If cattle bearing reservation brands were sold and then placed on ranges near the reservation there might be some question as to how they got there. This would be the case, particularly, if the original buyer had resold the cattle. Most of the cattle sold off the reservation went into feed lots, but certain classes – yearling heifers, and cows and calves – could be used to start or build up private herds.

At the time this study was being made bureau employees were still performing many of the duties during and in connection with the sales. However, tribal employees were taking over more and more of these activities.

Charges Against Sales Income

Each Indian cattle owner received money from the sale of cattle bearing his brand. However, before receiving his money he had to pay certain fixed charges and certain variable charges in connection with his participation in the cattle industry.

A resolution of the Tribal Council dated May 7, 1946, established the fixed charges:

> Whereas, after careful consideration and discussion the Tribal Council has decided that for the year 1946 a grazing fee of $2.00 per head will be charged on the sale of any and all calves under the age of six months and
>
> Whereas, a fee of $5.00 will be charged on the sale of all cattle six months or over
>
> Be it therefore resolved that we, the Council of the San Carlos Apache Tribe, establish the above fees for grazing for the year 1946.

These fixed charges were in force right down to the time of this study. In the last part of the above resolution these fees are referred to as grazing fees. They have also been referred to as sales fees and roundup fees. Such money has gone into tribal funds and has been used for hiring stockmen and line riders.

One of the important charges against the cattle owner, the branding fee, varied according to whether or not he participated, personally or by means of a substitute, in his association's roundup. If he did not, he was required to pay a penalty of $5.00 for each calf receiving his brand. These fees were deposited in the association's funds to pay operating expenses of the association, such as hiring range hands, purchasing salt and various roundup supplies, as well as making range improvements. In 1955 one of the associations raised the branding penalty fee to $10.00 per calf, and other associations were considering making similar increases. Even this increase did not reach the amount suggested by Saunderson (1952:9), the range consultant, who commented:

> In theory, each livestock owner in the associations takes an active part in the work and management of the livestock operations of his district. There are those cattle owners who do not, however, participate in the work and the management. Such owners are charged a calf branding fee of $5 per calf, by the association, for the work. In view of the present cash operating costs of stock ranches, varying from $30 to $60 per year for each head of cattle operated, the $5 calf branding fee is a very nominal charge. It probably should be at least $20, to

"stimulate" more interest by the cattle owners who let others do the work.

One Apache cattleman said that he had not been on a roundup since 1934. The following conversation then ensued.

"What happens when you don't go?"

"They make me pay $5 per head branded. But I haven't been paying anything."

"Why not?"

"Because I haven't had any branded."

Additional charges paid by the seller, which would vary from year to year, were: inspection, auctioneer, and feed for stock in the sale pens. Another charge was based on a resolution of the Tribal Council dated October 15, 1946, which established "a compensation fund for the care and maintenance of tribal employees and employees of any tribal association, injured in line of duty." This fund was being maintained at that time by a payment of 10 cents per head sold each year, but in 1955 the charge was 25 cents per head. Through the years, officials of the BIA have questioned the legality of this compensation fund.

Another charge against a cattle owner's gross income which had to be cleared up before he received a check was the balance due on his account at the tribal stores. After each sale a cattle owner was allotted a certain amount of credit per month, based on his net income from the sale of his cattle. In 1955, the amount of credit allotted an individual was determined by a group consisting of the Tribal Stores Committee and the managers of the two tribal stores. Any individual's account with the stores had to be cleared before he was issued a check for the sale of his cattle, and before he was given a new credit allotment. This gave rise to a statement frequently made, "Why should I work on roundup, the cattle belong to the store."

Distribution of Cattle Income

After the various charges had been deducted from a cattle owner's gross sale income, he received a check for the balance.

The same thing held true for the associations. Many, if not most, of them had accumulated charges on their accounts at the tribal stores. In many of the past years some of the smaller associations found it necessary to borrow from tribal funds in order to carry on their cattle operations. These accounts had to be cleared up before the association could draw any income from the sale of mavericks and from the branding fees.

An attempt was made in 1949 by one of the associations to distribute its net sales income on a per-capita basis to its members. An amendment to the association by-laws was passed by the members of the association. The Washington office of the BIA expressed strong objections to the amendment. The files at San Carlos do not indicate whether or not the distribution of funds was made.

Association and Tribal Expenses

At this point it is well to recall that the income for a cattle association consisted of the branding fee paid by owners who did not participate in the roundup nor provide a substitute worker; the proceeds from the sale of mavericks bearing the association brand; any assessments the members might see fit to levy. The tribal income from the cattle industry consisted of the grazing fee paid on each head of cattle sold; the small fee per head sold paid into the compensation fund; the proceeds from the sale of cattle from the IDT range.

The expenses of an association included the purchase of salt blocks for the range, and various roundup supplies. If cowboys had to be hired at roundup time, the association paid them. If range riders were kept out on the association range during the year, the association paid them. When a fence between two associations needed repairs, the expenses were split by the two groups. In general, the costs of range improvements were borne by the association making the changes.

The Tribal Council took the responsibility for a number of expenses related to the cattle industry. An item in the file entitled, "Tribal Relations," dated June 6, 1947, states that the tribe was paying the salary of a clerk handling tribal accounts in the agency office. A letter written by the superintendent to the commissioner in December, 1949, in regard to the handling of dividends proposed by one of the associations for its members states, "The Tribe does pay the salaries of two Civil Service employees at this office who handle and make such payments. . . ."

In 1954 the tribal government was paying the stockmen and line riders. A bureau official explained that when the associations were established they had no funds, therefore, the tribe paid those key range personnel. In April, 1945, a Tribal Council member recommended that the commissioner be requested to place all Indian stockmen on Civil Service and pay them from Indian moneys, with the tribe reimbursing this fund annually. In 1946 the board of directors of one of the associations recommended to the Tribal Council that their stockman be given a raise in pay, and the council agreed. In February, 1942, a member of one of the smaller associations reported to the council that the association's exterior boundary line needed a line rider. In 1946 a line rider on the northern boundary of one of the northern associations asked the council for a raise in wages, and his request was granted. An officer of one of the associations employed a line rider in 1947 without the consent of the Tribal Council. His association was required to pay the line rider from the date of employment to the next meeting of the council.

The minutes of the Tribal Council in April, 1946, show that "the Council agreed to use Tribal and Association funds to build houses for line riders." In regard to rebuilding a line rider's house, the minutes show that in October, 1950, "The Council agreed to put up one-half of the expenses out of S-100 fund and the Tonto Cattle Association will stand the other half of the expense if agreeable." However, other expenses involving range improvements were paid entirely out of tribal funds. The August, 1951, minutes state that a "washed out pipe line on the Tin Cup range will be repaired at the expense of S-100 fund." Also, the "middle pasture at Point of Pines will be repaired at the expense of I.D.T. fund." In June, 1948, "the Council agreed to clear out the drive way or stock trail through Yellow Jacket." Another type of tribal expense is indicated by the statement in the minutes for April, 1946, when "the Council agreed to the purchase of a truck for the I.D.T. herd and a pickup for the Registered Herd use."

As pointed out earlier, a tribal compensation fund was built up over the years by contributions per head of cattle sold. From this fund payments were made to men who were injured while participating in a roundup. A few examples drawn from the minutes of the Tribal Council show the nature of these payments. In 1946 one of the line riders was injured and confined to a hospital for a time. He applied for a relief grant from the council. The latter group passed a resolution "that Mr. —'s hospital bill be paid from Tribal funds and that he be allowed relief in the amount of $50.00 per month until he returns to his job as line rider on the San Carlos Apache Reservation." In the fall of 1946 an Indian who was injured while working on roundup demanded $500.00 from the compensation fund. He was paid only $51.00 from the fund, "and since there was no medical certificate showing his injuries he was not qualified to receive payment from the Compensation Fund and his demand was put aside to await further information." The minutes for January, 1948, show that "the Compensation Fund was to reimburse Clover Cattle Association on account that Clover Cattle Association paid $18 to ———, who was injured in line of duty." In the summer of 1954, a young Apache who had a leg in a cast said that his horse had thrown him during roundup the previous fall, resulting in a compound fracture of his leg. He said he had been getting payments from the compensation fund since the accident. The fund even paid funeral expenses in a few cases. In one instance, "the Council agreed to allow reimbursement from the Compensation Fund, built up by Indian cattlemen, to ——— for the funeral expense of his son and also to ——— who paid for the funeral expense of ———. Both men died in camp."

Through the years, the council made loans to associations to enable them to pay operating expenses between cattle sales. One such action included the stipulation that "the Directors of these two cattle associations are to sign promissory notes for the amount borrowed for a term of six months and pay interest at the rate of 4 per cent per annum."

Entering the Cattle Business

The articles of incorporation and by-laws adopted by the various associations in 1937-38 did not state qualifications for becoming a member of an association, or for continuing in that status. However, the Tribal Council seems to have retained the final judgment as to who could enter the cattle business or increase his holdings.

For some years after the organization of the cattle associations it was the practice for a man to start his son in the cattle business by giving the son some of his cattle, or buying a starting herd for him. Somewhere through the years this custom was eliminated and a man was no longer able to help his son get started. The files available at San Carlos do not indicate the date when this change took place. An entry in the minutes of the Tribal Council meetings dated January, 1947, states that "a new program for the issuance of cattle was discussed. . . ." In February of that year the council discussed the necessity of taking definite steps to cut down the number of cattle on the overstocked ranges. On April 1, 1947, the council approved a resolution which said in part that "no Indian family shall be permitted to graze over 70 head of breeding cattle. . . ." Also, on that same date there is a statement in the minutes that "the Committee to select 10 boys from Bylas and 10 boys from San Carlos who are to get issue of cattle this spring is to be named from the Council." Furthermore, the booklet describing the San Carlos Indian cattle industry, issued for the sales in the fall of 1948, includes the statement that "new owners who wish to go into the cattle business, apply to the Tribal Council for an issue of yearling heifers" (1948:4). Thus, it is likely that the change in policy regarding the starting of a young man in the cattle business was effected during 1947, although no resolution nor ordinance establishing the new policy was located.

The minutes for August, 1945, show that "the Council agreed that returning veterans should be given every help to secure loans to assist them in establishing themselves in the cattle business or any other business they might wish to engage in on the reservation." A bureau official said in 1954 that veterans had first preference, but that they were usually sons of cattle owners. However, in that same year the extension agent stated that a man could not start his son in the cattle business. He said that the young man must make formal application which was then to be processed through the proper channels described below. A number of cattle owners who were questioned about this matter were unanimous in agreeing that a man could not start his son in the cattle business. Most of them were rather philosophical about the situation, but a few were somewhat bitter.

In 1954 there was a definite routine to be followed in the processing of an application to start in the cattle business. The applicant sought the informal approval of the board of directors of the association he wished to join. If successful, he obtained the application form from the office of the extension agent and completed it. The form was then presented to the board. After formal approval by that group, the application was processed, in order, by the chairman of the Tribal Council, the bureau forester, and finally by the superintendent. Thus it can be seen that the real final decision on an application rested with two bureau officials — the forester and the superintendent. The forester was involved in the application procedure because at that time he was the official who set the carrying capacities of the ranges. The Apaches who were asked about this routine of applying to start raising cattle agreed that the steps outlined above were correct.

Much of the time there was a considerable waiting period between informal approval by the association and actual placing of cattle on the range. This endless waiting was a deep source of irritation to potential cattle owners. Some individuals sought direct action by the council. That the council was not always consistent in its decisions regarding these matters is evident from numerous entries in the minutes. Apparently that body was taking into consideration mitigating circumstances in certain cases.

In 1945 an applicant for a loan to purchase cattle was refused on the grounds that he had received an issue of cattle previously and had not taken care of them. Essentially the same thing is recorded in 1949. On the other hand, in 1946 the wife of a serviceman sought permission to start in the cattle business. She was referred to the board of directors of the association she wished to join. In addition she made a deposit of $200.00 in the tribal office. Later in that year she reappeared before the council where she was advised to record a brand and told that then she could buy her cattle. In 1948 a young Apache woman was permitted to buy 20 head of cattle, and early in 1949 another woman who applied to the council was also permitted to buy cattle. In 1949 two men who were officers of different associations were granted permission to buy additional cattle. On the other hand, in May of that same year an Apache woman seeking council approval of her acquisition of cattle "was told she would have to wait her turn," and the following July a man asking the council for permission to run cattle on the reservation "was told to sign up for it on the list and wait his turn."

In February, 1950, an Apache requested permission of the council to give his son 10 heifers to start a herd. "The Council advised that this procedure had been stopped because of the confusion among the cattle owners, so his request was denied." Later in that same year a man told the council that "he was unable to work and since he was in desperate need, he asked to be issued some cattle. He was told to wait his turn." About the same time another man applied for cattle, and it was agreed by the council that a specified association would "take care of him with their mavericks."

In 1954 it seemed to be the rule that only a man who was 21 years of age, or more, *and* head of a family could get started in the cattle business. A single man did not have a chance. This was vouched for by the extension agent. One of the Apaches also said, "Only married men can get into the cattle business."

Ash Creek, the largest association, was said to have a waiting list of 300 in 1954. One young cattle owner, while commenting that Apache boys are quite interested in raising cattle, added that "they have to get on the list and wait for an opening, so some of them get discouraged." Other Apaches, some of them cattle owners and some who were on the waiting list, referred to the same feeling of discouragement.

Once an applicant's turn had come he could select his cattle from one of three sources: the registered herd, the IDT herd, or mavericks bearing an association brand. The new owner would add his brand to whichever one was on the animals he secured. The herd from which he selected his cattle depended in part on his desire and in part on the stock available in the source herds. There was considerable difference of opinion among Apaches as to which source herd provided the best cattle for range purposes. One cattleman commented, "Well, mavericks will go to water wherever it is. Registered herd cattle are too lazy. IDT cattle are more like mavericks, they're wild. That IDT is rough range, it's hard to roundup cattle over there." When asked whether or not mavericks are good cattle, a young cattle owner replied, "No! They're wild. You never catch 'em on roundup." Another young Apache was asked where he got his cattle, and he replied, "From the registered herd. They're gentle cattle. They're the best." One young cattleman who got his cattle from the registered herd said, "I would rather have mavericks, they are more accustomed to range conditions. I don't think my cattle from registered herd have done too well."

The number of head of cattle issued to successful applicants has generally been 20. However, for some period of time following World War II, 30 head were issued. One informant said he received 20 head of cattle in 1945, another said he received 30 head in 1946, and a third young cattleman said he received 30 head in 1949. The sales booklet for the fall of 1948 stated that successful applicants received 30 head. It would appear that the change from 20 head to 30 head apparently took place in 1946. The files available at San Carlos did not establish the date of this change. Regarding the change back from an issue of 30 head to 20, there is a notation in the minutes for December, 1950, that members of the Tribal Council thought that the "issue of stock should go back to 20 from 30," but there is no indication of action at that time.

The financial aspect of receiving an issue of cattle could be handled in one of three ways: pay cash for the issue; get a loan – occasionally from the Tribe – to pay for the cattle; or receive the stock on a repayment basis. It was the third manner of acquiring cattle, on repayment, which involved most of those entering the cattle business. Those who entered under this plan were obligated to repay one head in addition to each ten head issued to them. Thus, during the period when 30 head were issued to a newcomer in the cattle business, he was required to repay 33 head, in a period of seven to eight years. During most of the years, when only 20 head were issued, the repayment consisted of 22 head. One young Apache cattleman, who had received 30 head, said that he turned in cows for repayment, saving the heifers for his herd. Another young owner stated that he got a loan from the Tribal Council to buy his cattle. The system of repaying cattle seems to have been a general policy of the BIA on other reservations where the Indians raised cattle.

Estate Cattle

Very early in the development of the San Carlos Apache cattle industry it became evident that the disposition of cattle belonging to a deceased Indian would constitute a difficult problem. A resolution passed by the Tribal Council in 1938 pointed out that a survey revealed that 25 percent of the cattle on the ranges belonged to estates, that nearly half of the Indian families were without cattle, and that the reservation was stocked to capacity. The resolution concluded: "Be it therefore resolved that estate cattle, as they are rounded up, be sold, and the proceeds divided among the heirs, according to their rightful shares."

Superintendent McCray wrote (1941:6-7) that the 1938 survey

> showed only 400 out of 700 family heads owning cattle. These estates created a situation which was a real menace to the continuity of the cattle industry. Because of their undivided share, heirs refused to contribute their proportionate part of labor on roundups. Members of associations, on whose ranges estate cattle ran, resented this situation. They felt that the heirs were deriving an income without effort. The result was that many calves were not branded and the number of mavericks was increasing on all ranges.
>
> . . . This condition was causing considerable worry. After lengthy discussion and consideration of various plans, the Tribal Council passed an ordinance ordering the sale of all estate cattle. The disposition of the estate cattle released grazing for those 300 families who were without cattle. The transfer from estates to active live members added to the working strength of the associations and at the same time eliminated the maverick evil.

The resolution concerning estate cattle did not prove to be a solution for the problems mentioned by McCray. The sale of estate cattle did release grazing areas, but it did not result in all the 300 family heads entering the cattle business. Those who did start cattle raising added somewhat to the "working strength of the associations." Contrary to McCray's hopes and expectations, the provisions of the resolution did not eliminate "the maverick evil." This was still a very serious problem at the time of this study. The difficulties caused by estate cattle are discussed in more detail in the next chapter.

Other Tribal Resolutions Regarding the Cattle Industry

Through the years the Tribal Council passed a number of resolutions and ordinances pertaining to the cattle industry. Five of the more important ones are mentioned below in chronological order. Comments by Apaches and BIA personnel pertinent to any of these council actions are included.

Twenty-Calf Limitation

In April, 1944, the Tribal Council passed an ordinance concerning those owners who were not eligible to sell cattle. The main part of the ordinance read, "Whereas it was proposed that no individual cattle owner who branded less than 20 calves in any one year should have the right to sell any heifers or cows, and the proposal was accepted." In 1954 the extension agent said that the ordinance was still in effect. He said that the ordinance represented an attempt to keep a breeding herd of reasonable size, at least until repayment cattle had been turned in.

Minimum Age for Range Hands

A very brief resolution was passed by the Council in September, 1945. It said simply that "no boys under 17 years of age shall be allowed to work on roundup on the Reservation." There was no comment regarding this resolution in the files, nor did anyone interviewed comment about it. However, a recheck of the association by-laws signed by members in 1937 and 1938 showed that Article II, Section 2, contains this statement: "Owners of brands unable to attend roundups may employ a person to represent them at the roundups, but this person must be 18 years of age or older." Perhaps the resolution served as a reminder and also to reinforce the statement in the by-laws.

Branding of Mavericks

An entry in the minutes for June, 1947, states that "the Council agreed to draft a resolution prohibiting the branding of mavericks by an individual, and anyone found guilty and convicted of such will lose all rights to cattle [run cattle] on the Reservation." A search of the appropriate files at San Carlos failed to reveal a copy of any such resolution. However, the association by-laws signed in 1937 and 1938 state, in Article II, Section 2, "All mavericks found on the ——— range shall be branded with the association brand." The blank line is for the name of the association. Thus, again, there seems to be a reinforcing device for a statement in the association by-laws. This was probably necessary because of the fact that periodically there was pressure from Apache cattlemen to revoke this regulation.

Seventy Head of Breeding Stock

On April 1, 1947, the Council passed a resolution establishing minimum ages for owners of cattle, and limiting the number of breeding head of cattle per family. This resolution states that only those Apaches "who are 21 years of age and older, or 18 years of age if married and the head of a family, shall be eligible to run cattle on the reservation ranges." Apparently there never was a great deal of opposition to this provision. But there was considerable opposition to the other major regulation established by this resolution which states, in part, that "no Indian family shall be permitted to graze over 70 head of breeding cattle. . . . In those cases in which both the husband and wife own cattle, the combined breeding herd shall not exceed 70 head of cows of breeding age." The greatest weakness of this resolution was the statement that "this Resolution shall be enforced by the combined efforts of the Tribal Council, the Boards of Directors, and the Superintendent and his employees." This gave practically everybody — tribal officials and bureau personnel — responsibility for enforcing the resolution, but in actuality did not concentrate responsibility anywhere. Since the 70-head limit was quite evidently unpopular with the Apache cattlemen, no one of the people charged with responsibility was willing to assume it, and there developed a very adroit game of "passing the buck."

In 1954 the extension agent said that one difficulty involved in enforcing the 70-head limit was the fact that cattle owners did not know how many head of cattle they had on the range; that the only count available at roundup time was the count kept in the extension office. But even if the owners had known how many head they were supposed to have on the range, there would still have been the problem as to who would enforce the rule.

The following opinions regarding the enforcement of the 70-head limit were expressed by two Apache cattlemen:

> ". . . the ordinance does not say who shall enforce it, the association, or the Tribe, or the stockman . . . or the Superintendent. You try to get a man to cut down on his cattle, and the roundup is over and he hasn't done that."
>
> "The ordinance regarding 70 breeding head is not enforced. Many have more, many have less."

There has been some question as to whether or not 70 head of breeding stock would provide a sufficient and satisfactory economic unit. Several people, both Apaches and bureau personnel, have given sets of figures to prove that 70 head of breeding stock are, or are not, a satisfactory economic unit. Since these figures differ widely and do not seem to include some rather important facts in some instances, they will not be presented in this report. However, it is worthwhile to note some of the comments regarding this topic. A bureau official stated that "if an owner worked his 70 breeding head properly each year, he could support himself and family on stock holdings with that basis — 70 breeding head."

Some of the opinions of Apache cattle owners are shown in the following conversations and statements.

"Can a man support his family on 70 head of breeding cattle?"

"I don't know, I guess so."

"Do you?"

"No. But if a man has 70 head of breeding cattle and gets 70 calves I guess he can make a living."

"Yes, but I understand that 80 percent calf crop is about all one gets."

"I guess that's right."

"I don't know whether 70 breeding head would support a man and family or not."

"Do you think a family can make a living just from cattle, if they have 70 head of breeding cows?"

"I don't think so. Maybe it depends on how many there are in the family. Now I have ten in my family, including my wife and myself."

"Can you support your family on 70 breeding head?"

"No!"

"If a man had two children, could he make it on that many?"

"I don't know. Maybe so. But I have eight children."

"Can a man make a living from the 70 head of cattle set by Tribal ordinance?"

"No, I don't think he can. Maybe just a man and his wife, but not if they have very many children."

"Do you make a living from your cattle?"

"Yes, but I don't have very many children any more."

"Could a man support a family on 70 head of breeding stock?"

"It's 75 head. He couldn't to begin with, but he might if he took care of them."

It is quite evident that the Apache cattle owners who expressed themselves on the matter took a rather dim view of supporting a family on the 70 head of breeding cattle. In fact, their statements implied that they were not supporting their families on this limited number of cattle. A very large majority of the cattle owners did not have anywhere near 70 head of cattle altogether, much less 70 head of breeding stock. In most cases the owners had income from other sources such as jobs, relief, or relatives. In a few cases individual owners had many more than 70 head of breeding stock grazing on reservation ranges. Since the only inventory of cattle on the reservation ranges was kept in the extension office, it would seem that a BIA official would have had to take the initiative in enforcing the 70-head limit. However, with all due respect to the extension agent's inventory of cattle, the fact remained that practically all of the individual owners had no idea how many head they had on the range. Only a few owners kept fairly good records of their cattle operations.

Failure to Work on Roundup

Two members of the council mentioned a resolution which apparently stated that if any owner did not work on roundup for two years in succession, his, or her, cattle would be sold. Undoubtedly, the rule still applied here, that any cattle owner unable, or unwilling, to participate in a roundup could send a substitute to work in his place. It proved impossible to find a copy of this resolution in the files at San Carlos. In regard to this resolution one council member and cattle owner said: "Sure it was passed but there are no teeth in it. Who is going to make them come out? They still won't come out." The other member of the council who was also a cattle owner said, "No cattle have ever been sold when they don't work. Tribal Council members are afraid they wouldn't be re-elected. ———has cattle, but has not worked for seven years. When it was threatened the cattle would be sold, a member of the family living off the reservation said the family would sue — so, no action."

It is obvious that these resolutions and ordinances, designed to make the Apache cattle industry operate more efficiently, failed in their purpose mainly because they had no "teeth in them." They looked fine on paper, but they did not work. Either there were no penalties stated, or the responsibility for enforcing the penalties was not centered on any one person or position. So far as the Apaches were concerned, there definitely were political aspects to be considered in enforcing these actions by the Tribal Council. In 1954 the office of councilman carried with it a definite and respectable income. With income being generally low and uncertain at that time, a member of the council, especially one with a family, would think twice before attempting to enforce one of these resolutions or ordinances.

Intergroup Contacts Related to the Cattle Industry

All of the actions and activities related to the cattle industry, as outlined in this chapter, came under the purview of the Tribal Council. In regard to the responsibilities of the council, the Constitution of the San Carlos Apache Tribe says, "It shall act in all matters that concern the welfare of the tribe, and shall make decisions in this regard that do not go beyond the limits set by this Constitution." Among the specific powers of the council were: conservation of assets, management of the tribal herd, passing of ordinances regulating voluntary associations. Thus, the constitution made it possible, and mandatory, for the Tribal Council to retain jurisdiction over all aspects of the cattle industry on the reservation. The reader has only to look back at the titles of the several sections of this chapter to get an idea as to the many aspects of the cattle industry which have been affected by council action, such as ordinances, resolutions, and various types of decisions.

Tribe and Associations

One important relationship between the tribe and the associations was the loans made to the latter. Some associations were involved in this relationship more frequently than the others.

A second relationship which involved the tribe and the associations was the fact that the tribe has paid the stockmen and the line riders.

A third aspect of this total relationship was the occasions when the tribe and an association worked together to make a necessary construction or emergency repair on the association range.

A fourth relationship was the joint meeting of the Tribal Council and the boards of directors of the associations. These meetings were held rather infrequently in the past, usually called to discuss a specific matter.

Interassociation Relationships

The data presented previously in this chapter have indicated that there were relatively few matters on which there were interassociation relationships. One thing mentioned specifically which required interassociation cooperation was the repair of a fence between two associations.

In 1954 two of the associations involved in a dispute over the control of a pasture were advised by the council to get together and come to an agreement.

The minutes of the Tribal Council state that in May, 1950, an association on the San Carlos Reservation entered into an agreement with a livestock association on the Fort Apache Reservation. "This agreement pertains to the cattle trap located at Warm Springs on Black River, the party of the first part desiring to install water gap and gate so stock water will be available on both sides."

Associations, Tribe, and Bureau

In general the associations took up their problems with the Tribal Council. However, the boards of directors and individual owners maintained fairly steady contact with the office of the extension agent. Association budgets usually were worked out with the extension agent. Also, boards of directors and individual owners went to the extension office for a wide variety of information and assistance. It should also be remembered that the only inventory of cattle on the reservation ranges was kept in the extension office.

The Tribal Council and tribal officials relied very heavily on BIA personnel for assistance in operating the Indian cattle industry. The superintendent and extension agent bore most of the load, but every department head was called upon for assistance, and some of them rather frequently. This dependence on bureau personnel was particularly heavy in connection with the cattle sales. One superintendent refused to sign the bills of sale for cattle, claiming that he had no authority to do so. Another superintendent expressed the opinion that more authority should be delegated to the associations, rather than concentrating so many decisions regarding the cattle industry in the Tribal Council.

Watering cattle during a roundup drive on the Point of Pines range.

Some members of a livestock association branding a calf.

Mavericks make roundup and management more difficult.

The headquarters and roundup crew at Charley Well.

6 PROBLEMS OF THE INDIAN CATTLE INDUSTRY

One of the purposes of the interviews and informal conversations with Indians and non-Indians was to determine what they thought were the problems of the San Carlos cattle industry. In the following pages, an attempt has been made to group related problems, rather than to discuss them in any order of importance. Some idea of the relative importance of any one problem will be indicated by the nature and extent of the discussion devoted to it.

Failure of Cattle Owners to Participate in Cattle Operations

Article II, Section 2 of the original by-laws for each of the associations contains the following statement:

> There shall be assessed a branding fee of five dollars ($5.00) per head in all cases where the owner of the brand is not present, or is not represented at branding time, unless sickness keeps him from being there, in all cases where a brand is represented and where the owner of said brand is not drawing compensation for his employment at the roundup, no fee or charge shall be made. However, exceptions may be made by the Board of Directors.

In 1942, shortly after the formation of the cattle associations, a field official of the Bureau of Indian Affairs who was in charge of the Indian cattle operations wrote to a similar official regarding the San Carlos associations that

> as they now exist, some of them must hire help to work the cattle, which is an unnecessary cost, which should be saved by each man doing his share.

The following item is included in the minutes of the Tribal Council meeting for September 4, 1945:

> Owners of cattle must report on roundups or furnish a man in their place. The practice of collecting a branding fee from owners not represented is resulting in many taking this way to get their work done. It is impossible to get adequate help unless cattle owners get out and do their share of the work. The end of the war and return of men now employed off the reservation will relieve the situation.

In 1954 the extension agent, who directed the cattle operations on the San Carlos Reservation, pointed out that one of the associations had increased the branding fee to $10.00, and that other associations were planning to do the same thing. He felt that even $10.00 was inadequate.

A number of the Indian cattle owners were asked about the extent to which members of their respective associations turned out for work on the range. The following are a few of the replies:

> "We have one of the largest associations, but only about six men ever come out to work on the range. The rest never come out, just pay the $5.00 penalty per head."

> "No, the owners don't come out to work. We have to hire fellows to do the roundup."

> "Maybe there has been enough money so that boys who are not interested don't have to come out to work their cattle."

> "Members think they own a piece of the reservation and as long as they pay their $5.00 a head it is all right if they don't work."

It is quite evident that the failure of owners to participate in the range work has been a very serious problem. This point will receive further discussion in Chapter 9.

Subsidiary to the general problem of an owner's representation at roundup is the matter of age of the representative. Turning once again to the by-laws of the associations, Article II, section 2, there is the statement: "Owners of brands unable to attend round-ups may employ a person to represent them at the round-ups, but this person must be 18 years of age or older."

This rule apparently was modified by a resolution passed by the Tribal Council on September 4, 1945, which states that "no boys under 17 years of age shall be allowed to work on roundup on the reservation." It was unofficially stated that this represented an attempt on the part of the associations to conform to the child-labor laws. This is also in line with the state law which requires that a youth must go to school until he or she is 16 or has finished the eighth grade, whichever comes first. However, in this regard there is a tribal ordinance which requires Apache youths to attend school until they are 18, because of the age retardation of Apache students in relation to non-Indians. Probably the Apaches, or their non-Indian mentors, or both, felt that roundup work is a man's job. Also, there might be a tendency for boys under 17 to "run" the cattle more.

Horses for Range Work

One reason frequently given by cattle owners for not participating in roundups and other range work is that they do not have any horses. It is true that the great majority of cattle owners do not have horses. On the other hand, it was pointed out in a council meeting in 1950 that "some people are not members of associations but still they own some horses and do not have cattle or range assigned to them." This emphasizes the problem of where to keep horses. In the same council meeting there was this further statement regarding horses:

> The chairman stated that every member belonging to various associations is supposed to keep his horses in his own association or is entitled to keep two horses if he feeds them and keeps them in pens.

From time to time an association has set aside part of its range for horse pasture. Also at times, the Tribal Council acting on behalf of the tribe has established horse pastures. In December, 1950, the Tribal Council took the following action:

> . . . it was suggested that land north and across the river from the residence district be set aside and it was agreed to do this, and the president of the Ash Creek Association said they would allow this land to be used as a pasture for the people who have no cattle. However, the title of this land will remain in the Ash Creek Association and permission must be obtained from the Ash Creek Association before placing horses in this pasture.

Two of the supervisory officials for the San Carlos cattle industry expressed somewhat different points of view in regard to the supply of horses available for range work. The stockman of the Ash Creek Association said:

> "I have just been over around Pine and Payson looking for horses to buy. I couldn't find any worth buying. I wanted to get them for the Ash Creek Association. But the only ones around are one-eyed or worse. They should have kept the horse range they used to have, and then sell horses to associations and members."

In a conversation with the extension agent, it was pointed out that several people connected with the cattle industry had indicated that there was usually a lack of horses for range work, and particularly for roundups. His comment was: "Oh well, you know, they would never have enough, but actually they do."

Two of the younger cattle owners said in regard to the availability of horses for range work:

> "I had four horses when I started in the cattle business. Now I have only one old horse. But I used to lend my horses to fellows going on roundups so I didn't get charged a fee."

> "There are enough horses for roundups. The Clover Association owns some horses. I used to own a horse, but not now. There used to be a lot of wild horses on the Clover range. If a man could catch any, he could put his brand on them."

One of the older men commented briefly in regard to the number of horses available, "Yes, I think there are enough. The association has some, and some members have some."

One middle-aged owner had his own ideas as to what should be done about the horse situation:

> "I would like to train the half-broken horses that are on the various ranges. Lots of the associations and members need good cutting horses. I would like to train boys to handle horses – they don't know how – then they could train others."

All these comments seem to point to certain difficulties in regard to the supply of horses: (1)

failure to maintain a sufficient supply; (2) shortage of well-trained horses; (3) lack of well-qualified cowhands; (4) failure to provide adequate horse pastures. One thing is certain, without an adequate supply of horses, and good horses, it is practically impossible to carry on range work, which means that the cattle industry deteriorates. Why should there be this basic failure in the Indian cattle industry?

Rough Handling of Cattle

One of the most common complaints regarding the operation of the Indian cattle industry, voiced by both Indians and non-Indians, was that the cattle are handled too roughly, particularly at roundup. One middle-aged Apache commented:

"I have worked as a cowboy for the Y Ranch, up northwest of the reservation. I go there after roundup here and work in the roundup there. I've picked up some information regarding cattle raising there. Five cowhands there handle 600 cattle. They don't 'holler' at the cattle, but drive them easy. Indians 'holler' at cattle too much."

Three other Apaches said:

"If the owners would work, there would be fewer mavericks. They would see their own cattle and brand the calves. Boys paid for the roundup work are interested only in the money. If they see a cow go over a hill, they don't go after her. But just riding and roping isn't the answer to a better cattle industry – this makes them wild. Another thing, we should establish weaning pastures."

"These cowboys run the cattle too much. I have worked cattle on the Fort Apache Reservation, but down here they run the cattle too much. Why it's just boys that work on roundup here and they really run the cattle hard."

"The country on this reservation is rough, the fellows that come out to work on roundup don't know the country. The mavericks are wild like deer, but these Indian cowboys don't know how to handle any cattle."

An elderly cattle owner gave a somewhat different point of view:

"At one time I worked for the Double Circle outfit. The foreman was a man by the name of John. He was a mean man, he sure was tough. He wouldn't let you rope calves for branding, you had to drive 'em into a corral and catch 'em by the hindlegs. He said that roping 'em made 'em wild. . . . No, I don't think Apache cowboys run the cattle too much. That man was just mean."

The opinions expressed by the first four cattle owners seem to represent the thinking of many Indian cattle owners. One trouble seems to have been that the owners of cattle who did not go out on roundup often were able to hire only the younger men, really late teenagers, to take their places. These younger men, full of vim and vigor, and lacking in training in handling cattle, probably did run the cattle rather severely. This involved yelling, or "hollering," at the cattle. Coupled with this is the fact that if a cow and a calf disappeared over a ridge or into a heavy thicket, there was no attempt made to secure the animal, thereby stimulating the development of mavericks. A large proportion of the range country on the San Carlos Reservation is very rough and broken, making it extremely difficult to work cattle, particularly at roundup. Also, the range within the boundaries of any one association is mainly open range. This, alone, makes it very difficult to control the cattle. When you add to these factors the youth and inexperience of many of the cowboys working at roundup time, a somewhat chaotic situation results.

Entering the Cattle Business – Interest and Opportunities

When the problem of entering the cattle business on the San Carlos Reservation was discussed, the younger Apaches expressed themselves very definitely. Furthermore, some of the older Indians Indians agreed with them. Following are some of the comments:

"Oh yes, most of the boys are interested in owning cattle in some association."

"Yes, there is a lot of interest, but where can the young Apaches go? They can't get in anywhere."

"Yes, there is an interest on the part of Apache boys to get in the cattle business. There are some waiting to get in each association. They try to go where their relatives are."

"Indian boys are quite interested in cattle raising nowadays. But they have to get on the list and wait for an opening, so some of them get discouraged."

"I think there is quite a bit of interest in the cattle business among the young men. I'm not too sure though, because there are quite a number of applications on file."

"There are lots of young men on the list of applicants. Some would be good cattlemen, some would not."

"Yes, there are boys waiting to get into my association. I don't know how many, but quite a few."

In 1954, the extension agent, one of the officials who had to process applications, said, with regard to applicants, "There are about 256 on the waiting list now. Some of them are very bitter about this."

Bureau officials who were charged with the responsibility of establishing the carrying capacity of the ranges on the reservation in terms of animal units grazing throughout the year were caught in a squeeze. On the one hand, they were required to establish the carrying capacities of ranges. On the other hand, they were subjected to severe pressures and criticisms from the Indians who desired to increase the number of cattle on the ranges, thereby increasing the number of cattle owners. They were also subject to pressures from some cattle owners who wished to increase their own holdings rather than permit new owners to come into existence. Many of the young Indians were very bitter about the fact that they could not secure permits to operate cattle on the reservation ranges.

Training for Cattle Raising

Some of the young cattle owners stated very positively that they wished they had received some real training in the handling of cattle. Some of them wanted a definite training program. The following comments by two of the young cattlemen are fairly representative of the others.

"The only training I got was what I picked up at the Y Ranch. . . . I would have been very much interested in more training, but nobody gave any."

"The only advice I got was from my brother-in-law. . . . There was no stockman for the association when I started out. There is now, but there wasn't then. . . . Yes, the stockman is supposed to help fellows like me, but there wasn't any then. They're supposed to help you in raising cattle. What to sell and what to keep. But I know more now. When my brother-in-law died, no one helped me, all the other cattle owners were too interested in their own cattle to help me. . . . I sure would like to have some training. But I would do better in the cattle raising now, if I could get a re-issue."

The extension agent felt that it would be a good thing if more of the younger Apaches would work off-reservation on cattle ranches. He thought they would gain valuable experience and bring back new ideas to the reservation.

The older men who expressed opinions on this matter of training looked at it quite differently.

"If boys want to learn the cattle business, they can hire out as cowboys and learn from watching the older men. When I was younger, they didn't make the boys stay in school so much, so sometimes I worked in the roundups in the fall or spring."

"The stockmen and foremen on the ranges are there to help young men learn."

"I don't know why these boys should complain about not getting training. They can go out and work on roundups and learn by watching the experienced men and by helping. They don't learn anything by sitting around."

"Even if men can't start their sons in the cattle business now, they can still train them. Or the boys can go out on roundup and watch how cattle are handled. They can go out any time and watch and learn how it's done."

"My father trained me to ride and to handle cattle. Boys don't get that these days. But they need some training."

This matter of training constitutes, unquestionably, a very real, and very serious problem. One of the fundamental ideas which caused the establishment of the associations was that relatives would be together and would aid each other in the cattle business. This included the training of the boys and young men. But, as time went on and the reservation ranges became stocked to capacity, a young man desiring to enter the cattle business might have a better chance of getting into some association other than the one in which he had relatives. As this situation developed more and more, it came to be the duty of the association stockman or foremen to give advice and training to the young cattle owners. However, as one of the informants indicated, some of the associations — especially the smaller ones — either did not have a stockman, or shared a stockman with another association. In the case of a stockman serving two associations, he did not have much time to give to the training of young cattlemen. The stockman of one of the larger associations said: "By the time I take care of all the duties that *have* to be done, including bookkeeping and paper work, I don't have a minute to give to these young cattle owners."

Here, then, is a very basic and very serious problem. Looking at it from a purely human point of view, the solution of this problem could lead to the solution of some of the other problems of the San Carlos cattle industry. The operations personnel of non-Indian cattle ranches are very thoroughly trained, and follow a very carefully planned system of range practices. If this is necessary for non-Indian ranches, it is equally necessary for the Indian cattle industry. For most of the families on the San Carlos Reservation, the cattle industry is *the* source of income. Therefore, this industry should be operated as efficiently as possible. The solution to this problem would be to provide as complete and thorough training as possible for those who are seriously interested in the cattle business. This might be accomplished by the tribe providing actual field training under well-qualified men during the roundups. For boys in high school this sort of training could be provided under simulated conditions during the summer months. Also, arrangements could be made for those young men who seemed best qualified to get additional training on non-Indian cattle ranches in central or southern Arizona. This very basic problem of the cattle business merits the most serious consideration of the people on the San Carlos Reservation.

Estate Cattle – Starting Sons in Cattle Business

As mentioned briefly in the previous chapter, it was thought that the 1938 resolution of the Tribal Council would solve the problem of estate cattle. In a letter to the commissioner on January 14, 1939, Superintendent McCray hopefully predicted:

> The sale of estate cattle will . . . effect a much better distribution of the cattle than now exists . . . it will permit the tribe to make a number of issues which will increase from year to year until all the families on the reservation will have cattle in individual ownerships.

Despite McCray's prediction, at no time have "all the families on the reservation" owned cattle "in individual ownerships." But the general policy did increase the number of families owning cattle. On September 5, 1941, McCray reported to Commissioner Collier:

> The disposition of estate cattle provided for a 20 head issue to the 300 families who owned no cattle. To date, over a hundred of these families have purchased 20 head each of young cows or heifers.

But the resolution did not solve all the problems. For one thing, the rule of selling the cattle of a deceased owner was not followed consistently. Minutes of Tribal Council meetings indicate that immediate circumstances were sometimes considered in deciding upon the disposition of estate cattle. In 1945 the wife of a deceased cattleman asked the council to allow her to retain half of the cattle of her late husband. In justification of her petition she stated that "she used her own money for purchase of part of the cattle." Her petition was granted. In the case of a cattleman who died in 1946 the council agreed "that what cattle were left on the reservation should be assigned to his son, who is now in the Army." And an entry in the minutes for September, 1950, states:

> The Chairman brought up two estate cases. . . . It was agreed that A's would be disposed of, but Mrs. B submitted a written agreement which was approved and signed by the Secretary of the Interior to retain the cattle in her name.

The policy of selling estate cattle met with various kinds of resistance. In 1950 one of the cattlemen stated to the Tribal Council that he had been in the cattle business for over 25 years. He also told the council that he did not favor disposing of estate cattle since that left the heirs with nothing. He insisted that the resolution concerning disposition of estate cattle be revised. Another point of view was expressed by a young cattleman who said, "In the sale of estate cattle some very good cattle are lost to the reservation." During the course of this study considerable pressure was being applied to the council to change the resolution so as to take care of the widow of a cattleman. However, no action of this kind had been taken by the council.

Coupled closely with the sale of estate cattle is the matter of a man wishing to start his son in the cattle business with some of his own stock. In the minutes of the Tribal Council meeting there is the following entry dated February 7, 1950:

> C requested the Council for permission to give his son ten head of heifers to start a herd of cattle. The Council advised that this procedure had been stopped because of confusion among the cattle owners, so his request was denied.

In 1954, regarding the starting of sons in the cattle business, the extension agent commented:

> "A man cannot start his son in the cattle business. But sons are given preference if they are on the list anywhere. Veterans have first preference, but usually are sons of cattle owners."

Some of the cattle owners made statements in regard to this aspect of the cattle industry.

> "I'd like to start my boy in the cattle business but I can't because there is a Tribal Resolution against it. . . . That's so you don't get too many brands in one family. There is supposed to be just one brand in a family. So when a person dies his brand is barred out and his cattle sold as an estate."
>
> "A man can't start his son raising cattle. The boy must apply and get on a list."
>
> "A man can't start his son with cattle. The son must apply for an issue of cattle. His father's cattle are sold as estate cattle."

The data presented above in regard to these two related problems suggest two points that merit discussion.

This writer did not find in the files at San Carlos copies of Tribal Council actions – resolutions or ordinances – in regard to these two problems. However, it is quite evident that the Tribal Council did take such actions.

One of the weaknesses of this aspect of cattle operations on the San Carlos Reservation was pointed out by one of the informants – the loss of good cattle to the reservation. If the cattle could be passed from a deceased person to one son or daughter, there is no reason why the cattle could not continue to operate under the same brand, or even under a modification of that brand. However, the difficulty seems to have been that all of the sons and daughters wanted a share of the estate cattle. That would have made for chaos. No one of the new owners would be willing to work all the cattle bearing that brand. It was suggested that the old brand could be barred out and new brands placed on the animals going to the new owners. In this regard, it should be pointed out that the barring out or modification of old brands can lead to some tricky and unethical practices. This loss of good livestock was delayed by allowing transferral of the permit, and the cattle covered thereby, to the spouse of the deceased. But at the death of the spouse the cattle had to be sold.

The second point that merits discussion is the idea expressed by Superintendent McCray but undoubtedly accepted by many others. In January, 1939, he said in reference to the sale of estate cattle that such action would make it possible that "all the families on the reservation will have cattle in individual ownerships." Such thinking is based on the assumption that all Apache families would, and should, be successful in the raising of cattle. Some of the proponents of this idea might have pointed to the fact that in pre-reservation times all Apache families engaged in the annual cycle of hunting and gathering. However, it should be pointed out that aboriginally the Apaches carried on subsistence activities as extended-family groups. Within any one of these extended-family groups there were simple or nuclear families – the type of family that we have in our society – with some of them being less successful in those subsistence operations than the balance of the group. Nevertheless, if the Apache people were to exist, then hunting and gathering had to be carried on by some portion of the population. It is true that the ancestors of the Western Apaches did some small-scale farming. But here it is even less likely that all nuclear families were successful. It is the nuclear family that Kitch, McCray, and many others through the years have been trying to make into successful cattle-raising units. It is this writer's contention that there is no reason to expect that every Apache nuclear family would be successful in raising cattle. After all, it is a well-known fact that many of the Navajo nuclear families do not even attempt to raise sheep, and yet it is customary to think of the Navajos as a tribe of shepherds. With the opportunities that the Apaches have had for wage work – and other sources of income – in recent years, there is even less reason to expect that they would all be successful in the cattle industry.

It is this writer's belief that those Apaches who are seriously interested in making a living from the cattle business should be encouraged and aided in doing so. They should pay a reasonable return to the tribe each year for the privilege of using reservation resources for their cattle operations. Those who are not able to brand a reasonable number of calves each year, and who are obviously not seriously interested in the cattle business, should be required to withdraw from the cattle industry, since they would not be in position to pay the tribe as a whole a reasonable return for the use of tribal resources.

Mavericks Versus Registered Herd

There was some difference of opinion among cattle owners as to whether it was best to start with mavericks obtained from the associations, or with high-grade stock from the registered herd. Three of the cattlemen interviewed on this subject were in favor of the mavericks, and five favored cattle from the registered herd. The three in favor of mavericks said:

> "They're rather wild. But mavericks will go to water, wherever it is. Registered herd cattle are too lazy."

> "I got my issue of cattle from the registered herd. But I would rather have maverick cattle, they are more accustomed to range conditions. My cattle from the registered herd have not done too well. At the registered herd, they get the eggs mixed up and produce yellow cattle, off-color cattle."

> "I got my cattle from the registered herd, but I think mavericks may be better. They are tougher and can forage for themselves better."

Some of the points made by those who favor an issue of cattle from the registered herd are:

> "You see my issue was all mavericks. They're too wild. They run into the brush when they see you. Maybe some mavericks are gentle, I don't know."

> "I got 20 head of mavericks. They were on Ash Creek, but I lost most of them. Mavericks are wild like deer. Most of them are wild, but maybe some are good."

> "I got my issue of cattle from the registered herd. They're gentle cattle, they're best."

> "Apaches should get their cattle from the registered herd. They're gentle and all are good cattle now."

> "Mavericks are secured from the associations. But they're too wild. You never catch them on roundup."

One of the older cattle owners said:

> "We should have weaning pastures. We must gentle the cattle. Mavericks are pretty hard-headed. If owners would work, there would be fewer mavericks, they would see their own cattle and brand the calves."

In discussing the maverick problem one of the officials of the BIA indicated his position in this controversy in an indirect way.

> "Mavericks should be watched more closely. This means more men working at roundups. Maverick mothers are likely to have calves that will grow up to be mavericks, both hightail it for thickets when men and horses show up. I think they could be tamed by leaving salt and meal and coming back with more later."

At the time this study was made, opinion on the San Carlos Reservation concerning this problem was probably very much in the same ratio as indicated in the above statements. Among those people at San Carlos – both Indian and non-Indian – who seemed to know the cattle industry rather well, it was generally conceded that mavericks constituted a very serious problem. As pointed out by those who favored mavericks, they are hardier animals in general, better able to forage for themselves, and more likely to find water. But, because they are so wild, the returns to the owner are much less than from gentler stock. The hardier maverick, even though wild, would appeal to the type of cattle owner who is not sufficiently interested to put in time on the range working his cattle. If cattle from the registered herd are put on the association open range, they must receive more attention, but the owner benefits tremendously at sale time.

Issues of cattle were sometimes made from the IDT or commercial herd. These cattle have tended to be somewhat wild, because the IDT range, located in the far southeastern part of the reservation, is rather rough and broken. It is very difficult country in which to work cattle.

Repayment of Cattle

No matter whether a new cattle operator draws his issue of cattle from the mavericks controlled by an association or from the registered herd there must be repayment. This can be made in terms of cattle or cash. Statements by a few of the younger cattle owners indicate how this works:

> "I got 30 head in 1946 as a veteran. This was a repayment issue. I repaid 7 this year, and I think I have about 3 more to repay. I turn in cows for repayment and save the heifers for my herd."
>
> "I got my cattle in 1949. I got a loan from the council to buy the cattle. I got another issue last year to build up my herd. I will repay 22 head for the 20 head I got."
>
> "I received 20 head from IDT 2 years ago on a repayment basis. I will repay 22."
>
> "In 1926 I got 20 head of cattle and paid for them in cash as I could. But I lost most of them later. Later I borrowed $700 and got 20 head of mavericks on Ash Creek."

Under the cattle repayment plan, 11 head of cattle must be returned for each ten head received. This means that if the issue were 20 head, then 22 head must be returned. If the repayment is in cash, it must be in terms of the average market value. But there seems to have been some difference of opinion at times as to whether this "average market value" should be as of the time of the issue, or at the time of cash repayments. The average market value does fluctuate from year to year, and even throughout the year, and a person making repayment in cash always wants to do so at the lowest possible value. Where the repayment has been in terms of cattle returned, the owner has had a maximum of eight years in which to make the repayment.

The other way to get an issue of cattle has been to secure a loan from the tribe, from an association, or from outside sources, and sign a note for the amount borrowed.

This matter of repayment, whether in cattle or in cash, has become very complicated. It requires well-trained personnel to handle the business intricacies. The entire cattle industry should be under the over-all supervision of a general manager of tribal enterprises, who should oversee a manager of the cattle industry.

Number of Cattle Owned

Having acquired an issue of cattle there was the matter of keeping account of these cattle and the natural increase from them. Under the existing conditions, including very rough range country, it has been difficult for an owner who was seriously interested in the cattle business to know how many head he had. When to those conditions is added the lack of real interest on the part of many cattle owners, it is not strange that many of the owners did not know how many cattle on the range bore their brand. The various individuals interviewed were asked if they knew how many cattle they had on the range. The following three statements are sufficient to represent the type of answers given:

> "No, I don't know how many head of cattle I have."
>
> "I don't know how many cattle I own. I don't think anyone does."
>
> "I don't know, but I don't think I have any. Maybe three or four head."

There is no *easy* solution to this problem, but there is a solution. If an owner goes out to work on roundup, he is likely to see most of the cattle bearing his brand. He can also see the calves that mother up to his cows, and see that they are properly branded. This will give him a rather good idea of the total number of cattle that he has on the range. Then, by subtracting the number that he decides to sell, he knows fairly accurately how many cattle he still has on the range. However, he can obtain this sort of information only by working on roundup. Otherwise, he has to take somebody else's word for the number of cattle he owns.

Limits on Number of Cattle Per Person

On April 1, 1947, the Tribal Council, at a regular meeting, passed a rather lengthy resolution concerning the cattle business. One part of the resolution states that only resident and enrolled members of the San Carlos Apache Tribe who are 21 years of age and older, or 18 years of age if married and the head of a family, shall be eligible to run cattle on the reservation ranges.

However, the part of the resolution that has received the most attention, at least in terms of discussion, says:

> Be it further resolved that in accordance with a Tribal Council Ordinance of January 17, 1936, no Indian family shall be permitted to graze over 70 head of breeding cattle, including cows and heifers over 18 months of age, on the reservation ranges. In those cases in which both the husband and wife own cattle, the combined breeding herd shall not exceed 70 head of cows of breeding age. This resolution shall be enforced by the combined efforts of the Tribal Council, the Boards of Directors, and the Superintendent and his employees.

Two questions arise in connection with this part of the resolution: (1) Has this portion of the resolution been enforced? (2) Do 70 head of breeding cattle form a sufficient economic unit for a family? Answers to these two questions were sought from some of the cattle owners:

> "I don't know whether a man can support his family on 70 head of breeding stock or not – I guess so. I don't, but I've got a boy going to Haskell this year, and I've got a girl in Gila Junior College. But if a man has 70 head of breeding cattle and gets 70 calves I guess he can make a living. [*It was pointed out here in the conversation that an 80 percent calf crop is about the highest one could expect.*] I guess that's right. . . . The ordinance is not enforced because it does not say who shall enforce it, the association, or the tribe, or the stockman, or the superintendent. You try to get a man to cut down on his cattle and the roundup is over and he hasn't done that."

> "I don't think 70 head are enough. Maybe it depends on how many there are in the family. Now I have ten in my family, counting my wife and myself. If a man had only two children, maybe he could make it. I don't know. But I have eight children."

> "No, I don't think a man can make a living from 70 head of cattle. Maybe just a man and his wife, but not if they have very many children. He has to get a job then."

> "It's 75 head, not 70. A man couldn't support his family on that many to begin with. But he might if he took care of his cattle."

Two of the BIA officials connected with the cattle industry on the reservation did some calculations regarding the annual income that a man could get from 70 head of breeding stock. They arrived at somewhat different totals for the annual income, but both agreed that a man could make a living for his family if he worked on roundups. One of them said: "So, if an owner worked his 70 breeding head properly each year, he could support himself and family on stock holdings with that basis – 70 breeding head." This official figured that an Indian owner could have had a net income of $3,400 in 1954, if he worked on roundup.

Given these rather conflicting opinions between the Indians and the BIA officials, the next question, which neither of the two officials attempted to answer, is whether or not $3,400 is sufficient income for a family for a year. If so, what size family?

Actually, the debate as to the economic adequacy of the 70-head limit is somewhat academic, for two main reasons. Responsibility for enforcing this provision of the resolution was so widely dispersed among so many people that there was no one enforcing it. Out of 717 owners (or holders of permits) listed on the 1953 tally sheet of calf brandings, only 35 showed a *total* of 70 head of cattle. About half of these would have been steers. So those who had just over the 70-head total would have had much less than 70 head of breeding stock. Of the total number of individuals listed, 172 show no cattle at all in their brand. This brings up a point made earlier, that people who are obviously not making use, or even reasonable use, of their grazing permits should be removed from the cattle industry.

Cattle Associations

The following discussion of the possibility of consolidating associations is intended to be only a presentation of the historical background, because in 1956 several of the associations were consolidated.

There were really three problems involved in connection with the associations: (1) Were the associations the best way to handle the cattle business on the reservation? (2) Should the smaller associations be consolidated? (3) To what extent should the associations handle their own funds?

Indian cattlemen, both old and young, were asked to state their opinions regarding the efficiency of the associations as a means of operating the Indian cattle industry:

"I was very much in favor of the associations when they were started, and I still am. I think they are a good thing. If you are rich, you don't need the associations. But, for those who aren't, like me, the association is a good thing. Many cattle owners only have a few head. I think the associations are pretty good the way they are."

"I don't have much information about the associations. I'm not sure they're good, but I don't know anything any better."

"I think the associations are successful. I would like to run my cattle myself, I think I could do better with them. But the way it is, it has to be in associations. That's all right."

"Sure, the associations are successful. How else could we operate on a reservation? We can't as individuals, we couldn't have small enough plots. How would you find your cattle on the entire reservation?"

"I think associations are a success. Relatives can help each other on the range."

"Oh yes, I think the associations are a good way to handle the cattle business."

"If the reservation were dissolved, I would want my cattle on my own farm. But there are 900 owners now. There are not enough waterholes for each family to have one. I think the association is the better way, it makes the best use of range and water."

All but one of the cattlemen interviewed felt that the associations were all right, and probably the only way to handle the Indian cattle industry on the reservation. The one exception said that he was not sure about the associations but he could not suggest anything any better. Most of the individuals quoted above, and others who expressed opinions in the course of rather casual conversations, said that they could not see any other way to operate the cattle industry on the reservation. As one informant pointed out, it would be impossible for any owner to find his cattle if they could move freely over the entire reservation. This suggests a solution – reservation-wide in nature – which will be discussed later in this chapter. Only one person mentioned the matter of the number of watering places, but this is a very important point, for there are even now barely enough on the various association ranges. The point made by the first individual quoted, that many owners had only a few head, is theoretically linked to a point made by one of the other informants, that relatives could help each other. This was one of the basic ideas when the associations were established. As the associations developed through the years, this principle became less and less operative. But the principal point made by these informants, that there seems to be no better way of operating the Indian cattle industry than by means of the associations, remains true at the time of this writing.

The idea of consolidating the smaller associations to form larger and more efficient range units was discussed as early as 1945. From that time on to 1956 the idea was revived periodically and discussed pro and con. (The action that was finally taken in 1956 is discussed in Chapter 7.) That the smaller associations were not economically efficient range units is evidenced by the fact that the minutes of Tribal Council meetings for practically every year indicate that one or more of the small associations applied to the Tribal Council for a loan in order to carry on operations. On June 30, 1949, there was a joint meeting of the Tribal Council and the boards of directors of four associations – Circle Seven, Hilltop, Victor, and Cassadore – "to discuss the proposed plan of consolidating these four associations." The minutes indicate that many of the Indians present, as well as several of the bureau personnel, spoke on the subject of consolidation. This was a long meeting with much lively discussion, but no action was taken. During the years until 1956 this matter of consolidation was the subject of many official (and unofficial) discussions and official reports.

During the meeting in June, 1949, the Indians present were reluctant to take any action toward consolidation. In 1954, this writer was able to get definite statements from only two of the Indian cattle owners.

"I think some associations are too small, but nothing can be done about them. People in those associations won't change, they are friends, they know each other. If they did go together to form bigger associations, they wouldn't get along, there would be friction."

"I think that Hilltop, S.E. [Victor], Circle Seven, and Cassadore should become one association. They could make better use of their range winter and summer. But the members of some associations don't want to work with others."

The third problem concerned the fact that for some time after their formation the associations did not handle their own financial affairs. The general file on "Stock Raising, Cattle Associations" has the following entry regarding a joint meeting of the Tribal Council and the boards of directors of the associations:

> The expense of the cattle industry has in the past been paid entirely from the common fund known as S-100. Now, all associations are anxious to be allotted their share of this fund and their own association expenses. . . . The associations agreed that they should pay for all expenses from their own funds.

Commenting on this meeting and the decision referred to above, Superintendent McCray said:

> By throwing the responsibility for the proper management of their funds on the Directors I believe they will come to a point where they can handle their own affairs much quicker than were we to continue as in the past.

However, as mentioned before, the smaller associations ran into financial difficulties almost continually and appealed to the Tribal Council for loans, year after year. The San Carlos Withdrawal Report, dated September, 1952, calls attention to this problem.

> Livestock Association Boards of Directors and officers must be further trained and must have sufficient experience to be able and willing to accept full management of the association business . . . . insist that associations manage their own business and pay the costs of such management.

An idea concerning the reservation cattle industry which was mentioned several times in the course of casual conversations was that there be just one brand for the entire reservation. As it was discussed informally, this would amount to the setting up of a tribal corporation to operate the cattle business. Brands of individual owners would be barred out and the brand of the tribal corporation applied. Each individual would receive credit in the corporation for the number of head of cattle taken over. This credit would be in the form of stockholders' certificates, much like those of any commercial corporation. Indians who did not have title to any livestock would be permitted to buy shares in the corporation, particularly as the operations of the corporation expanded. Dividends would be declared annually in terms of so much per share. The people who handled various aspects of the cattle business would be employees paid by the corporation.

In the situations where this writer heard this plan discussed, it was only in the broadest of outlines. It was criticized by some, both Indians and non-Indians, because it would destroy individual initiative. Proponents of the idea pointed out that there was not much evidence of individual initiative among the Apaches under the existing situation. It was also pointed out that a large percentage of the Indian cattle owners were then receivers of dividends without much investment involved — usually none in terms of time and effort. The fact remains, however, that whatever its good and bad points might be, this plan has never been considered favorably.

Another idea that had been considered over the years was to eliminate the fee of $5.00 per head charged for each head of cattle sold. In most instances, it was suggested that a scale of grazing fees should be set up similar to those charged for grazing livestock on national forest land. One of the BIA officials said in 1954 that "the reservation grazing fees should be based on the fees charged for grazing on National Forests, about $1.25 per cow-month." Such a scale of grazing fees was included in the 1956 ordinance that changed many aspects of the San Carlos cattle industry.

Non-Indian Range Employees

In the general file on "Stock Raising, Cattle Associations," there is an entry written in longhand, and without any date; however, the other material in this file was dated 1938.

> We the members of the Board of Directors on San Carlos Indian Reservation dont want White Stockman but one. We like to get Indians to be Stockman. We dont want no White Stockman to run cars all the time. We want them to ride nothing but horses. We like to get them to use horses all the time and stay on the range, not down here. All the pickups ought to be taken away from them at once, if they want to hold the Stockman job.

The minutes of the Tribal Council under date of December 4, 1945, contain the following:

> Council brought up the fact that there were so many white men employed on IDT. . . . Advised that ——— was merely helping out during round-up for cattle sales, and has or would soon return to Horse Camp to break horses. This matter will be brought to attention of the Extension Agent.

The file entitled simply "Stock Raising" includes an undated statement by Superintendent McCray in which he comes to the defense of the white stockmen. Other items in the file all bore dates in 1940. Apparently, the Indians had just been attempting to get rid of all white stockmen. McCray said:

> They have been the backbone of the industry. When the Indians became discouraged, they encouraged them to stick with it until they succeeded. They have protected the Indians' interests against outsiders and against the Indians themselves.

In general, the Indian cattlemen interviewed by this writer did not say much about non-Indian employees in their cattle industry. Two of them merely pointed out that the stockman for each of their associations also served another association in that capacity. Thus, two stockmen were serving four associations. An elderly cattleman said a little about the duties of the stockmen:

> "They check on the cattle and watch the water traps, and keep salt nearby. In the winter they get bogged down sometimes. Even a horse will bog down in winter when it's snowy. We can't drive up there in the winter, the roads are too muddy. It's a lonely life for the stockman."

For many years following the establishment of the associations, the stockmen on the various association ranges apparently were non-Indians. During the ensuing years the ratio of Indian to non-Indian stockmen fluctuated. In 1954, only one of the seven stockmen was non-Indian. In the quotation from the undated item in the files there is the statement that the Indians want the stockmen (non-Indian?) to stay on the ranges, and not spend so much time down at San Carlos. The reader may remember that when the associations were established, Superintendent Kitch assumed that the Indians would move out onto the ranges with their cattle. This did not happen, and the Indians have been strongly criticized for not doing so. As pointed out by McCray and the elderly cattleman, the life of the stockman and other range employees is a lonely and difficult one. It has been difficult to get well-qualified men to take these posts. It seems that most of the Indian cattle owners have not been interested in spending much time out on the range, summer or winter.

Another problem in connection with the matter of non-Indian employees in the cattle business has been the inadequacy of range personnel through the years that the associations have been in operation.

Referring to the lack of an extension agent and the presence of 33,000 head of cattle on the reservation, Superintendent Kitch wrote to the Commissioner in March, 1937, that

> to accomplish this administration, we have four stockmen. Previous to this when the reservation was under permit to whites, this same area, with practically the same number of cattle, was handled by seven permittees, each having a separate manager drawing up to $5,000 per annum with a bonus. Each of these outfits carried annually from five to twenty paid white cowboys. We are now operating this range with four stockmen and about six Indian line riders supplemented by gratis the assistance during roundups by the Indians.

That the range personnel has continued to be inadequate in numbers has been made evident by the statements in the preceding pages of this report. A stockman sometimes served two associations. Furthermore, he might be the only year-around employee on the range. Numerous informants have been quoted indicating that the Indian cattle owners had not, and still were not, turning out to work on the roundups. Some of the associations did not have the funds to hire range hands to work throughout the year. This factor, along with the inadequacy of training of many of the men who did turn out for roundups, added up to very inefficient cattle operations.

Compensation Fund

One of the very real problems associated with range work is the possibility of injury to the men working on the range. This is particularly true at roundup when many, if not most, of the men have not had sufficient experience in handling horses and cattle. Men who had been injured during range work lodged claims for compensation and medical expenses with the Tribal Council.

In September, 1945, the council took action on the matter as indicated in the following quotation from the minutes:

> Chairman Clarence Bullis presented a plan to establish a fund for compensation of men hurt while working in the cattle industry. The proposition was that an additional dollar per head be assessed on all cattle sold this fall which would yield between $8,000 and $10,000. This fund would be available for payment of such compensations as might be approved. At the end of each calendar year an assessment would be made to cover the amount paid out during the year. . . . Details as to rate of compensation, period of payments, etc., were to be worked out by a committee appointed by the Chairman.

In October, 1946, a resolution was passed by the Tribal Council setting up such a compensation fund, with an annual levy of 10 cents per head sold. On August 10, 1947, the Tribal Council passed a resolution which rescinded the actions of previous resolutions relating to the compensation fund. While this 1947 resolution spelled out the matter in more detail, still it contained the statement that "the amount of ten cents (10c) shall be the voluntarily contributed amount for each head of cattle sold. . . ."

From time to time, officials of the Bureau of Indian Affairs have questioned the validity of the compensation fund. In the minutes of the Tribal Council for March, 1947, there is the following entry:

> A letter from the Office of the Commissioner questions the advisability and feasibility of the Tribal Compensation Fund set up in the Resolution of October 15, 1946. He suggests that it might be well to get information from private insurance companies regarding their underwriting some such plan.

At the time of this study, in 1954, the compensation fund was still in operation. The extension agent at that time said that the annual levy was 25 cents per head of cattle sold. With the reorganization of the San Carlos cattle industry in 1956 this fund was abolished. There seems to have been much opposition to the fund from Indian cattle owners, as well as from the Bureau of Indian Affairs.

Other Problems

Of the four remaining problems to be discussed here, two are based on criticisms made by Indians, and the other two on criticisms made by non-Indians.

One of the criticisms heard most frequently from the Indian owners, and used by them to justify their failure to do range work, is represented by the following statement.

> "A man can't make a living off cattle. He has to have some other work. The store takes all he can make from cattle. The cattle belong to the store."

The last sentence is the statement so frequently heard. A cattle owner will say essentially that his cattle belong to the store, so why should he go out and work them. Let the store take care of them. Certain facts should be presented here so that the reader may understand the background for this sort of statement.

The tribe owns a store at San Carlos and one at Bylas. Indians are allocated credit at these stores on the basis of the net amount of money resulting from their sales of cattle. Where an owner does not work his cattle, and the number of head decreases each year, the amount of credit available to him at the stores decreases. But the cattle owner considers it a personal affront when the stores decrease his credit. For the stores it is a straight business proposition — no cattle, no credit. The individual cattle owner considers it anything but straight business. He fails to realize that the stores belong to the entire tribe, to him and all the other Indians on the reservation. Nor does he realize that for the stores to stay in business they must not only break even, but must show a profit. For all too many years the Indian has had too much done *for* him. First, it was the federal government, then, in more recent years, he has turned to his own tribal government. He completely overlooks the fact that as a member of his tribe he shares in the responsibility for its solvency, which includes the stores.

The other type of criticism heard from Indians is essentially that there is too much government control. One man said:

> "The Indians should have control of grazing. Sometimes we have found feed for cattle, but the government insisted on reduction. Today, the people still don't want to be told how many cattle they can run. In our district the range looks much better than white men's ranges."

This is, of course, a specific protest against stock reduction and range control, protective measures remaining in the hands of local representatives of the Bureau of Indian Affairs. This is another instance of too much being done *for* the Indians and not enough *with* him. It seems reasonable to expect that if more Indians had been given more education, particularly practical education, on problems such as this, there might now be less resistance in solving these problems. On the other hand, there are people, both Indian and non-Indian, who say that Apaches would not follow the leadership of any of their own members on such matters.

Most of the non-Indians who have been associated in any way with the Indian cattle industry are convinced that the Apache people do not understand the problems of raising cattle, and do not show any interest, generally, in understanding those problems. But, perhaps, one of the best statements in this regard was made by one of the Indian cattle owners, who said:

> "It's a matter of education that the people don't come out to work. They don't understand the problems. They don't understand what work like installing the trough and trap at S. Spring means, they've never done it. That trap will catch lots of wild cattle, cattle the association doesn't know it has. But association members don't understand this."

If, as this Indian cattle owner said, it is due to a lack of education that the Indian people do not understand the problems connected with the cattle industry, then who should have done the educating, and who should have been educated, and how should this have been done? These questions are discussed in the next chapter.

The final problem will only be mentioned, not discussed. This problem is based on the critical statement by non-Indians that the Apaches do not know nor understand the proper values that should be associated with the cattle industry. This writer would like to point out that if we agree that the Apaches do not understand the value system associated with the cattle industry by non-Indians, then we must also agree that we non-Indians do not *really* understand the Apache value system. In a situation like this, judgments by either group are difficult to make, and are definitely tenuous.

7 REORGANIZATION OF THE SAN CARLOS CATTLE INDUSTRY

In Chapter 6 the problems that plagued the San Carlos cattle industry through past years were outlined. Now it is appropriate to state briefly what has been done to solve these problems.

Beginning as far back as 1945, advisory experts on range management and livestock raising pointed out the weaknesses of the cattle industry on the San Carlos Reservation and suggested changes to correct those weaknesses. Some of these recommendations were:

1. Combine certain of the 11 associations to make possible the maximum utilization of range resources.
2. Reduce the number of head of livestock on the ranges to the estimated carrying capacity.
3. Increase the calf crop through controlled breeding, earlier weaning, and other livestock management practices.
4. Build fencing to establish pastures for controlled grazing, and traps at water sources.
5. Eliminate mavericks by means of more fencing and gentler handling on the ranges.
6. Require associations to purchase range bulls.
7. Require all owners of livestock on the reservation to pay a grazing fee.
8. Employ a general manager for all livestock operations.

In 1956 the superintendent, members of his administrative staff, range personnel, Tribal Council members, and members of the boards of directors of the existing associations sat down around the conference table to discuss the problems of the Indian cattle industry and the possible solutions. A great many sessions were necessary in order to arrive at a mutual understanding of the basic needs of the cattle industry and the most efficient ways of satisfying those needs.

As a result of these cooperative conferences, the Tribal Council, in October 1956, passed Ordinance No. 5-56 to regulate the livestock industry and range management. Subsequent revisions of this ordinance made provisions for most of the criticisms of the Indian cattle operations which had been made by the advisory experts.

One of the principal criticisms had been that several of the associations were too small to be economically efficient. This had been shown by the fact that these associations were continually applying for loans for operating expenses. As a result of the 1956 conferences the 11 associations have been combined and reorganized into five associations – resulting in more efficient units. The following table shows the effect of this reorganization:

Former Associations	*New Associations*	*Date of Incorporation*
Cassadore Circle Seven Hilltop Victor	Anchor Seven	May 6, 1957
Tin Cup Tonto	Tonto	May 23, 1957
Slaughter Mountain	Slaughter Mountain	June 25, 1957
Clover Point of Pines	Point of Pines	August 16, 1957
Ash Creek Mohave	Ash Creek	December 7, 1957

In addition there are the following range units: the registered herd; the tribally-operated range in the southeastern part of the reservation known as the IDT, which provides funds for the tribal government; and a small range unit along

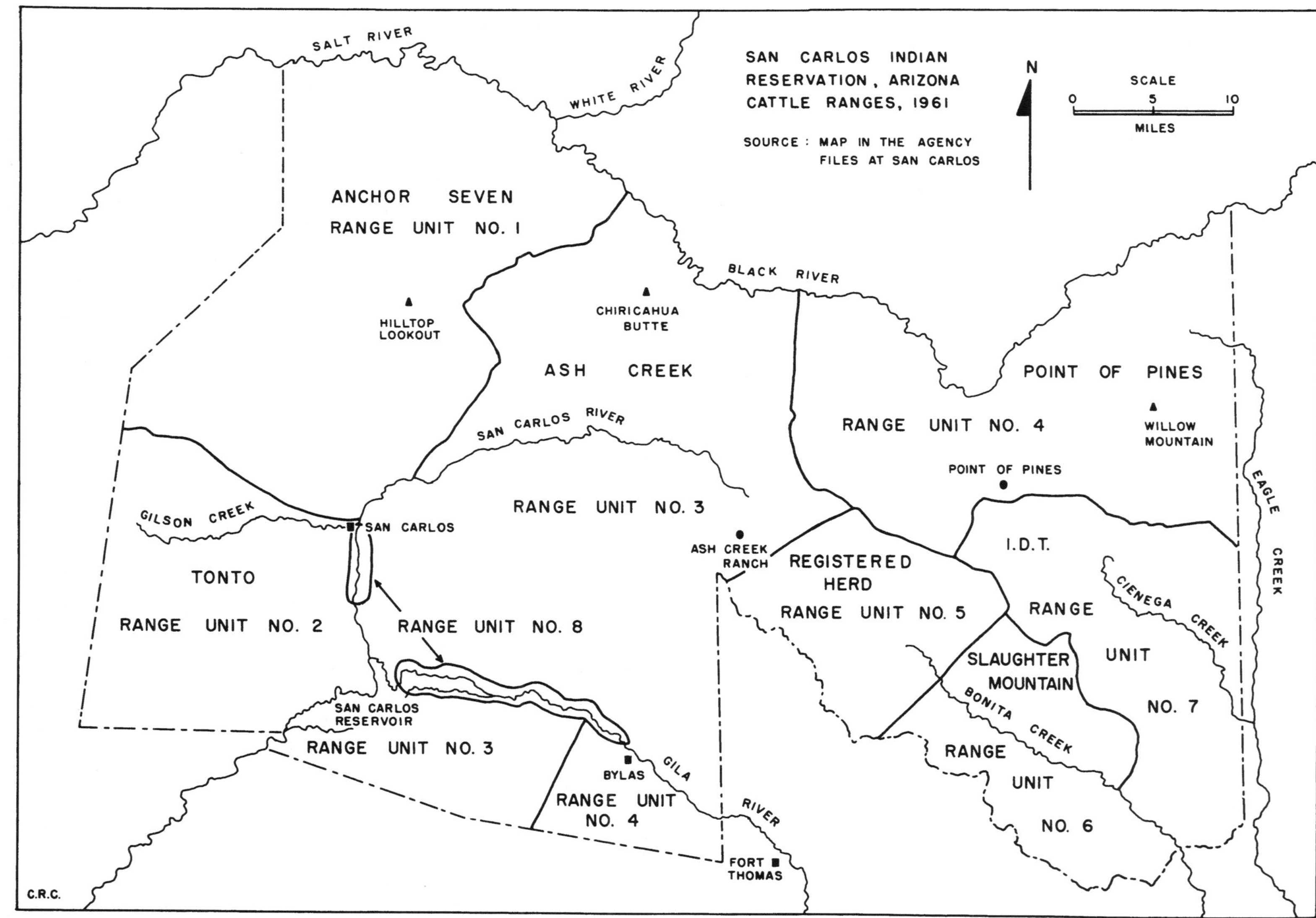
SAN CARLOS INDIAN
RESERVATION, ARIZONA
CATTLE RANGES, 1961
SOURCE: MAP IN THE AGENCY
FILES AT SAN CARLOS
N
SCALE
0 5 10
MILES
SALT RIVER
WHITE RIVER
ANCHOR SEVEN
RANGE UNIT NO. 1
HILLTOP LOOKOUT
CHIRICAHUA BUTTE
ASH CREEK
BLACK RIVER
POINT OF PINES
RANGE UNIT NO. 4
WILLOW MOUNTAIN
POINT OF PINES
SAN CARLOS RIVER
RANGE UNIT NO. 3
GILSON CREEK
SAN CARLOS
ASH CREEK RANCH
REGISTERED HERD
RANGE UNIT NO. 5
I.D.T.
EAGLE CREEK
CIENEGA CREEK
RANGE UNIT NO. 7
TONTO
RANGE UNIT NO. 2
RANGE UNIT NO. 8
SLAUGHTER MOUNTAIN
BONITA CREEK
SAN CARLOS RESERVOIR
RANGE UNIT NO. 3
BYLAS
GILA RIVER
RANGE UNIT NO. 4
RANGE UNIT NO. 6
FORT THOMAS
C.R.C.

the Gila and San Carlos rivers operated by the tribal enterprise, in connection with their feed yard, as a source of income.

As indicated above, the new associations have been incorporated under the laws of the state of Arizona. The associations can, and do, borrow money at banks in communities adjacent to the reservation. Cost accounting has been established for each association, with the result that the directors have a clearer idea of expenses. This enables them to draw up a sound budget for each year. The associations are in position to make needed improvements on their ranges, such as additional fences, development of water resources and construction of traps. Each association has regular monthly meetings of its board of directors. There is also an annual meeting of the members of each association. All of this means that the Indians are now operating their associations themselves.

The All-Directors Association, consisting of the members of the boards of directors of the five associations, is operating in a regular and functional manner, meeting every two months. Two of the most important functions of this over-all association are making recommendations in regard to the contract for the manager of livestock operations, and expenditure of funds for general livestock operations.

The manager of livestock operations is responsible for supervising all association activity on the reservation. Gradually this official is getting the Indian cattle owners to use better livestock and range practices. At sale time, under the supervision of the livestock manager, the Indians now handle all the preparations and procedures, such as dividing the sale cattle into classes, further dividing them into sale lots and placing them in pens, recording the sales, and aiding in loading the cattle on trucks or railway cars.

The Tribal Council in 1959 passed Ordinance 59-6 amending Ordinance 56-5, Article III, Section 6, Grazing Fee. That section now includes the following:

> Each livestock owner shall pay grazing fees for the privilege of grazing his livestock on the San Carlos Reservation in accordance with the following rates:
>
> Twenty-five (25) cents per month for each head of cattle owned, six months of age or older.

This payment is made to the association of which the owner is a member. In turn, the association pays to the tribe "grazing fees in an amount equal to $3.00 for each animal unit authorized in the terms of the grazing permit." Half of this payment is returned to the association to be put into its range improvement fund. The balance of the payment provides financial support for the tribal government. These fees are collected at the time of the sales in terms of the number of cattle sold. In effect, then, the grazing fee has become a sale fee, at least from the cattle owners' point of view.

Under the former system an owner was required to work on roundup, send a substitute, or pay a fine. Under the new system an owner is not permitted to work on the range in lieu of a fine, because there is no longer a fine. However, an owner of cattle may do range work as a paid employee. Each Indian owning cattle on a reservation range pays a year-long grazing fee of $3.00 per head for all animals over six months old that bear his brand. One half of this fee is returned to the association to be used for range improvement. The balance of the fee provides financial support for the tribal government. Each association pays all the men necessary to do range work, roundups, and drives to the sale pens. In this way, inefficient range hands can be eliminated.

Under the new system the associations are required to purchase their range bulls. Formerly, the range bulls were issued, essentially on a loan basis, from the registered herd. Gradually the Indian cattlemen and their associations are accepting the related principles of controlled breeding and earlier weaning of calves. This means that eventually bulls will be on the range with the cows only during certain seasons of the year. Weaning pastures are being established for calves. These practices have already resulted in some increase in the calf crop.

One of the main problems in connection with the San Carlos cattle industry has been the inventory of animals. Prior to 1958 the annual inventory figures were only estimates. Thus, the following figures show the apparent fluctuations in the total number of cattle more than 18 months old on the reservation ranges in the years indicated:

1945 . . .	28,241	1953 . . .	29,565
1946 . . .	38,567	1954 . . .	31,212
1947 . . .	35,139	1955 . . .	28,632
1948 . . .	30,767	1956 . . .	25,935
1949 . . .	31,600	1957 . . .	21,996
1950 . . .	29,564	1958 . . .	20,377
1951 . . .	29,809	1959 . . .	18,075
1952 . . .	27,532	1960 . . .	17,516

In order to make the annual inventory figures firmer, new inventory methods were tried. During the years 1959 and 1960, on three of the association ranges the cattle were rounded up as completely as possible, and these cattle were counted as they passed through a gate from one pasture to another. While they were confined, an airplane survey was made of the cattle not inside the holding pastures. The gate count was of cattle over the age of 18 months. The airplane count was also of cattle over the age of 18 months to the extent that this can be determined from an airplane. Even so, this was an attempt at a more accurate count, whereas the figures prior to 1958 were definitely estimates. The combination of gate-counting and airplane-counting showed that one association was actually below the estimated carrying capacity for its range.

One of the problems which it was hoped this study would clarify is the relationship between income from the cattle industry and total income for the San Carlos Indians. It proved to be impossible to determine this ratio, even approximately, but it was possible to secure figures for the gross income from cattle sales.

Year	*No. Sold*	*Gross Income*
1957	9,383	$1,131,576
1958	7,971	1,215,527
1959	9,216	1,197,462
1960	12,024	1,563,922

However, the difficulty lies in the fact that there is no way of determining the total income of the San Carlos Indians. The principal unknown item is the amount of income derived from off-reservation work, which is probably a rather large item. It has even been impossible to secure dependable figures for on-reservation income, since several sources are involved.

In order to see specifically how many of the goals suggested by the advisory experts have been achieved, it is best to analyze the results in terms of the eight points stated at the beginning of this chapter.

1. The 11 associations have been combined to form five associations in order to make maximum use of range resources and to improve business management in the livestock industry.
2. Stock reduction has been accomplished largely by small owners going out of the cattle business – selling whatever stock they had in order to meet credit obligations.
3. The practices of controlled breeding and earlier weaning of calves are being accepted by an increasing number of Indian cattlemen.
4. Gradually, more pastures are being established for controlled grazing, and more traps are being constructed at watering places.
5. A sustained effort to reduce the number of mavericks is providing the desired results.
6. Associations are now required to purchase range bulls.
7. All owners of livestock on the reservation now pay an annual grazing fee.
8. A general manager has been employed for all reservation livestock operations.

Much remains to be done in future years in improving the San Carlos Indian cattle industry, but much progress has been made in the last five years.

8 ANALYSIS

It is very evident that the development of the cattle industry on the San Carlos Reservation subsequent to 1932 involved directed culture change. Prior to that year there had been some small effort at directing change in this aspect of culture, but apparently most of the previous cattle-raising activity had been of a non-directed nature.

In terms of Linton's definition of directed culture change, the dominant white English-speaking group (referred to hereafter as Anglo) interfered "actively and purposefully" with the culture of the Indians on the San Carlos Reservation. Efforts were made to "inhibit the exercise of pre-existing culture patterns." The centralization of the Indians in two communities on the reservation under the control of United States military forces made it impossible for the Indians to carry on their former hunting-and-gathering subsistence pattern. The rationing system was an entirely new cultural complex with which the Indians had to become acquainted. This was also true of many of the Anglos charged with the responsibility of operating the ration system. However, with the operation of the rations system there was, for some period of time after establishment of the reservation, no concerted attempt to "stimulate the acceptance of new culture elements." At least in the area of subsistence, except for some supervised farming, there was no real effort made to stimulate the acceptance of new culture elements until shortly after the turn of the century. There was, then, a sort of delayed action in getting directed culture change into full operation. The old patterns of culture were inhibited, but due to the ration system no immediate effort was made to make the Indian self-sustaining.

In discussing the means of distinguishing between directed and non-directed culture change, Spicer (1961:521) emphasizes two criteria:

> To summarize, the decisive criteria for distinguishing the two major classes of contact situations may be indicated. (1) If definite sanctions, whether political, economic, supernatural, or even moral, are regularly brought to bear by members of one society on members of another, one condition for directed contact is met. (2) If, in addition, members of the society applying the sanctions are interested in bringing about changes in the cultural behavior of members of the other society, then both necessary conditions for directed contact exist.

At San Carlos, subsequent to 1932, definite sanctions, mainly economic, were brought to bear by the Anglos on the Indians. Constant pressure was maintained by the Anglos. Thus, it is easy to see evidence of Spicer's first criterion. Furthermore, the Anglos who were applying the sanctions were definitely "interested in bringing about changes in the cultural behavior" of the Indian society. The personnel of the Bureau of Indian Affairs on the San Carlos Reservation were responding to general pressures to put each American Indian tribe on a self-sustaining basis as quickly as possible. In order to accomplish this goal, they were attempting to get the San Carlos Indians started in the raising of cattle in an organized manner. Undoubtedly, it was felt by some Anglos that change in the subsistence aspect of the Indians' culture would lead to, or accelerate, desired changes in other aspects of their life. However, it is very likely that the majority of Anglos involved were primarily interested in changing only the subsistence aspect of the Indian culture at San Carlos. They probably gave no thought to possible changes in other aspects of culture which would occur if the Indians were induced to become cattle raisers.

It is true that efforts were made quite early to educate the Indian boys and girls in schools established on the reservation. Even with the concentration of the Indians on the reservation in two or three communities, success in educating the Indian youths came rather slowly. However, one factor making for more rapid culture change among the San Carlos Indians was the increasing availability of wage work, both on and off the reservation. The Indians involved in this work had money for purchases of Anglo goods.

It was pointed out in the first chapter that Linton defined several concepts which are very useful in understanding culture change. The first of these to be considered are the closely related ones of form, meaning, and function.

Form

Linton states that the form of a trait complex is "something which can be established objectively and through direct observation." If the form of a trait complex can be established through observation, then it also should be possible to state objectively the form of an activity such as the Indian cattle industry. It is, then, suggested here that the form of the San Carlos Indian cattle industry has been evident in terms of the following components.

1. The cattle on the ranges.
2. The ranges – forage and sources of water.
3. Owners, range hands, other personnel.
4. Techniques used in handling the cattle–roundups, branding.
5. Associations of individual owners – meetings, officers.
6. Sale procedures.
7. Income from sales; use of the income.
8. Range improvements, or lack of them.

These various components of the form of the Indian cattle industry can be seen to have been derived from the Anglo cattle industry. As has been pointed out in some detail earlier, the guiding hand of the Anglo is obvious in all the components of the form of the cattle industry.

Meaning

According to Linton's definition this concept "consists of the associations which any society attaches to it [trait complex]. Such associations are subjective and frequently unconscious" (1936: 403).

Difficult though it is to apply this concept to cattle raising generally, it should aid in distinguishing between the significance of the cattle industry to the Indians and to their Anglo mentors. The form of the cattle industry has been essentially the same for Anglos and Indians, with at least one very important difference. Whether the Anglo was operating as an individual cattle owner, or as the manager for a company, his motive was to make as much profit as possible. The income of the individual owner or of the company depended on maximum efficiency in the operations of the ranch. Otherwise, the annual income was imperiled. Furthermore, most Anglo cattle raisers were interested in being as successful as possible, because of the prestige factor involved.

The Indian cattle owner, however, has been a member of an association, under the guidance of some member of the reservation BIA staff. He could make decisions, but he did not have to do so. Generally speaking, income from cattle raising was considered by the Indians to be supplemental to income from other sources. If the income from his cattle sales was small or nonexistent, an owner would be able to get along. He might do wage work on or off the reservation. He could always fall back on the Bureau of Indian Affairs or the tribe, or other members of his extended-family group.

This concept of meaning takes one into the area of the values important to any society. It is the opinion of this writer that we do not understand sufficiently well the value-systems of the Anglos or of the Indians who have been in contact at San Carlos to be able to make sound pronouncements about the differences in meaning relating to the cattle industry. However, a few suggestions can be made which should be checked further to see how valid they may be.

One of the Indian values concerned subsistence. The pre-reservation life of these Indians required considerable, but mainly periodic, effort to secure mere subsistence. This means that the Indians were accustomed to value periodic rather than sustained work patterns, in keeping with their hunting-and-gathering subsistence activities. Then rationing in the early reservation period reinforced this value. Subsistence was provided and there was no incentive to work. Wage work, following the period of rationing, was seen by the Indians in terms of Indian values. The majority of the Indians were still subsistence-oriented. They worked long enough to get the money sufficient to buy things that were needed, or desired. Most of the Indians have carried this value on into cattle raising. The sustained effort necessary to raise cattle successfully – as proved by Anglo cattlemen – was not in keeping with the values of the subsistence-oriented Indian. All of the permit-holders started out with at least 20 head of cattle. But the sustained work necessary to maintain, much less to increase, these herds has not been a part of the value system of these Indians. Probably no more than a dozen Indian cattlemen have operated on a basis comparable to that of successful Anglo cattlemen.

Another, and closely related value for the San Carlos Indians was that of collective responsibility within an extended-family group. In pre-reservation times such a group carried on cooperative subsistence activities. Particularly in regard to hunting activities, if only one or two individuals were successful, all members of the group shared in that success. At another time someone else would be successful and again all would share. The two important points here are: cooperation within an extended family, and the ability of that group to exist satisfactorily on the successful efforts of only a few members at any one time. This state of affairs has carried on to the present.

Kitch and his assistants were aware of this extended-family unit, but apparently did not fully understand the nature of its operations. As each range group was established, its core consisted of one or more extended families which were recognized as having prestige. Other families of lesser prestige and with sometimes very little in the way of blood relationships involved attached themselves to the core families.

On these somewhat heterogeneous groups was imposed the Anglo formal association. The organization and operations of these associations were completely foreign to the Indians. Furthermore, the manner of organization of the associations stressed the individual, which was an Anglo value and in conflict with the Indian value of cooperative activity within a kin group.

The auxiliary principle involved, that of sharing the successes of group members, has generally meant that cattle, possessed by members of a kin group, or the profits derived therefrom, must be shared with other members of that group. This, along with the lack of sustained work habits, has tended to keep herds small, or to eliminate them. Here again, the Indian value of reliance on cooperative group effort is in direct conflict with the Anglo value on individual thrift.

Still another value of the San Carlos Indians is that of rather continuous sociability based on the concentration of the population in limited residential areas. In pre-reservation times the permanent winter camps were along the rivers. Rationing at army posts reinforced this pattern. This value has been strong enough to remain the major factor in keeping the Indians from moving onto the ranges with their cattle. Anglo cattlemen have usually lived on the ranges used by their cattle. This is necessary in order to provide the more or less continual care the cattle need. Kitch had this in mind when he proposed to have the Indian cattlemen move onto the ranges with their cattle.

Thus it becomes evident that Indian values have operated to prevent the Indians from having the felt needs in regard to their cattle industry that have been recognized by Anglos. The Indian values affecting the cattle industry have been in part: (1) a work pattern based on periodic activity; (2) stress on cooperation in kin groups; and (3) sociability based on concentrations of population. On the other hand, values important to Anglo cattlemen include: (1) sustained work habits, which imply the associated values of thrift and acquisition of capital for present and future needs; (2) stress on individual enterprise; and

(3) willingness to accept isolation in return for long-range gains.

These Indians found it neither necessary nor desirable to incorporate into their value system Anglo values of thrift and acquisition of capital. Down through the years these Indians had the benefit of directive paternalism from the federal government, and more recently from the tribal government, and even from the cattle associations. These forms of paternalism have given them a sense of security which they have been reluctant to lose.

Coupled with this conflict between values attached to the older Indian subsistence activities and the values necessary to successful modern cattle operations is a very important factor. This is the fact that the paternalistic activities of the Bureau of Indian Affairs personnel, and more recently of the Tribal Council, have tended to inhibit individual enterprise on the part of Indian cattle owners.

The over-all result seems to be that the great majority of the San Carlos Indians have accepted the cattle industry in terms of their existing cultural values, their meanings, rather than in terms of the Anglo values and meanings usually associated with this industry.

Function

> The use of any culture element is an expression of its relation to things external to the social-cultural configuration; its function is an expression of its relation to things within that configuration (Linton 1936:404).

The function of the San Carlos cattle industry must be seen in relation to the Indian culture if we are to follow Linton's definition. The culture of the San Carlos Indian began undergoing definite change with the establishment of the reservation and the settling of the Indians thereon. The subsistence pattern of hunting and gathering supplemented by small-scale farming was largely eliminated in favor of government rationing. When general rationing was abolished in 1904, the San Carlos Indians entered another new and different way of life, in which their livelihood was derived in small amounts from many sources – small-scale farming, work for governmental and religious personnel on the reservation, work as rangehands for Anglo cattlemen who were leasing reservation ranges, and gradually increasing amounts of off-reservation wage work. Cattle raising by the Indians did not assume any real importance until 1932. From that date on, as the Indian cattle industry expanded, it became increasingly important as a source of income for the Indians. The principal function of the cattle industry was to increase the economic base of the Indians. This stimulated change in other aspects of the Indian culture, notably in housing, clothing, household utensils, and transportation. It is the opinion of this writer that the development of the cattle industry had little, if any, effect on the socio-political structure and the religious system of these Indians. The socio-political structure of the Apaches had been shattered in the shifting around and concentration of the Indian population in the early reservation period. The formation of the tag bands was a powerful factor in this breakdown of the former socio-political structure, and the heavy hand of the superintendent and his staff in the early decades of this century essentially finished the job. The extended family is probably the only unit to have survived to any degree. The relatively simple religious system of the Apaches does not show any basic effects from the development of cattle raising. Beef has been used as an item in the food supplied to guests attending religious ceremonies, but this is primarily in the subsistence aspect rather than the religious.

Therefore, the function of the cattle industry has been primarily economic, effecting changes in the material trait-complexes. In that respect cattle raising has acted as an agent of change. However, the industry seems to have had no direct function in regard to the changes that have occurred in the socio-political and religious systems.

In the introductory chapter the question was raised as to whether or not cattle raising had become a universal characteristic of the San Carlos Indians. This was in reference to another set of concepts proposed by Linton – alternatives, specialties, and universals. According to this line of thought, new items may enter a culture and be accepted as cultural alternatives or be rejected.

Cattle raising was accepted. However, it was introduced as a specialty rather than as an alternative by the advocates of culture change, who hoped that cattle raising would become a universal. The facts are that cattle raising has been practiced by only a portion of the Indian families on the reservation. Since not all families have raised cattle, this means that the industry has not become a universal. As defined by Linton, a universal culture item is something like "use of a particular language, the tribal patterns of costume and housing, and the ideal patterns for social relationships" (1936:272). On this basis, the definite statement can be made that cattle raising became a specialty among the San Carlos Indians, but not a universal nor alternative.

The available data indicate clearly that some San Carlos Indians adopted cattle raising as a specialty and became relatively successful cattlemen. Why? What characterized this segment of the Indian cattlemen? Careful analysis of the available data has been made in terms of the following questions.

1. Were any of these men cowboys under the former White lessees?
2. Would they have been successful under any cultural pattern, and with any subsistence system?
3. Was it due to the fact that any one association had superior range?
4. Was there better management of the range of any particular association?

In an effort to answer the first question, 16 of the more successful Indian cattlemen were selected. This selection was based on the number of head of cattle accredited to each one on the 1953 tally sheets. Exactly half of the 16 are known to have been employed by one or another of the White lessees. It is likely, but not certain, that these Indians learned good practices in cattle raising during such employment.

In regard to these 16 men, the author finds it impossible to answer the question as to whether or not these men would have been successful if operating any other subsistence system. One may speculate about the matter, but where and how does one find the facts on which to base such an answer?

There is no doubt that the Ash Creek Association had superior range, because of its spread north and south and through various altitudes. This gave the cattle on that range ample seasonal forage and water. Because of their over-all high altitudes several of the association ranges, such as Point of Pines, Clover, and Hilltop had good summer ranges, but their winter ranges were less favorable.

Without more complete data than are available it is practically impossible to compare the management on any one association's range with that on the other ranges. This involves the extent to which the various associations were able to employ stockmen. It has been indicated previously that some of the associations, especially the smaller ones, shared the services of one stockman.

Empiricism

What about the factors that Erasmus (1954: 147-58) points out must be considered in analyzing a case of directed culture change?

Empiricism refers to changes that bear clear and short-term evidence of their effectiveness. The raising of cattle does not qualify in this respect, because the building up of a herd that produces a satisfactory income requires time and much effort. Even if the BIA personnel were aware of this need for short-term gains, the fact remains that real benefits were not immediately available. Because of this factor alone, many of the Indians were not interested in really becoming cattlemen. The history of rationing and governmental paternalism had conditioned them to look for immediate results. Many of them took their issue of cattle, but did little or nothing to increase the issue of 20 head. Some of the cattle issued were butchered in a relatively short time. Others became wild and disappeared into rough, brushy country.

Need

There is considerable question as to whether or not the San Carlos Indians either felt or recognized a need to develop a cattle industry. When Kitch proposed to remove the Anglo cattlemen from the reservation so that the Indians could expand their own cattle-raising activities, the latter, or at least many of them, protested the move. Their protest was based on the fact that they would lose the income from the grazing fees paid by the Anglo lessees. Probably the majority did not, at that time, feel any need or desire to improve their conditions by means of the income from cattle raising. The superintendent and his staff saw a need to get the Indians into the cattle business, but, in general, the latter did not. Most of those Indians who did become aware of such a need saw it and the cattle industry in terms of Indian values which did not place any premium on the sustained work necessary for successful cattle raising. It is likely that neither Kitch and the members of his staff nor his successors were aware of this value orientation on the part of the Indians. Therefore, through the years, generally, the San Carlos cattle industry has not been successful in terms of the standards prevailing in the non-reservation cattle business.

Spicer (1952:18) probably would see this failure on the part of the San Carlos Indians to develop a really successful cattle industry as resistance. He says this is "a symptom of something wrong in the cross-cultural situation," perhaps impracticality of the change, or unsatisfactory intergroup relations. Undoubtedly, there was some resistance to Anglo ideas in regard to developing the Indian cattle industry. However, there was a lot of plain indifference or apathy based on failure to recognize the need, and the lack of adequate short-term results. Perhaps we can think of this indifference as passive resistance.

Cooperation

An important factor involved in the failure of the San Carlos cattle industry to become a success was the lack of cooperative effort on the part of the agency personnel and the Indians. Too much was done *for* the Indian cattle owners, and not enough *with* them. This is a very time-worn statement, nevertheless it was very true in the development of the San Carlos Indian cattle industry. As indicated in previous chapters, some member of the agency, apparently the extension agent, supervised the activities of the Indian cattle industry from its beginning in 1932. During the years when this study was being made, the records concerning individual cattle owners and the associations were kept in the office of the extension agent. Any and all problems concerning the cattle were taken to him for solution. He made the decisions. Sales procedures were handled by the extension agent, assisted by members of the agency staff. The Indians, long accustomed to paternalistic efforts on their behalf by the agency, accepted the situation. Coupled with the failure to recognize a need and the lack of adequate short-term results, this failure to stimulate cooperative effort on the part of the Indians and the agency led to a lackadaisical attitude toward cattle raising on the part of most of the Indians.

As pointed out in Chapter 6, due to recent cooperative discussions which included Indians and agency personnel, a revised system of Indian cattle operations has been adopted. Because of this cooperative planning the system seems to be working very well in 1963. The associations are taking full responsibility and making their own decisions. This is the result of cooperative planning.

Inducement

In the introductory chapter it was pointed out that if any proposed change is carefully and cooperatively planned, there should normally be little or no need for inducement measures. However, where a faulty system, such as the San Carlos Indian cattle industry, was operated for such a long time with little or no effort to induce improvement, and with people well conditioned to that system, a period of retraining and reorientation would be necessary. At San Carlos real efforts at inducement began with the recent cooperative discussions at the agency and Tribal Council level. From that point on it has been a matter of each convert to the new program selling additional cattle owners.

Complexity

As a final item involved in situations of directed culture change, Erasmus calls attention to the matter of cultural complexity. In this case, the cultural activity undergoing change, the cattle industry, is very complex itself.

However, Erasmus is referring to the complexity of the relationships between this cultural activity and all aspects of the San Carlos Indian culture pattern. As pointed out earlier in this chapter, apparently the only real culture changes effected by the development of the cattle industry were in the more material elements of culture and in providing a helping hand in the further breakdown of the social organization. These recent changes in the operations of the San Carlos cattle industry would seem to indicate the development of another change, a willingness to accept Anglo values in regard to sustained work on the ranges by trained personnel. This change, which has taken a long time to develop, has undoubtedly affected other values, and probably other aspects of the reservation culture pattern which are not immediately evident.

It should be fruitful to examine the development of the San Carlos cattle industry in terms of the four "stages" of cultural transition outlined by Vogt (1951:88-89).

Vogt's first "stage" represents the kind of contacts which existed on the San Carlos Reservation in the early years. There was minimal contact with Anglos and probably most of the aboriginal value system still governed the lives of the Indians.

The next "stage," the imitative, with its increased effective contacts with Anglos, made it possible for selected aspects of the dominant culture to be imitated but not internalized. This has certainly been true of the San Carlos cattle industry throughout most of its years. The Indian cattlemen went through many, though not all of the motions characteristic of the Anglo cattle operations, but they attached their own meanings to the industry. This is what Linton meant when he said that the form might be accepted, but then coupled to meanings current in the receiving culture. It is suggested here that this imitative "stage" may be characteristic of all situations of culture change where paternalism in any form may be present. The term paternalism here refers to the roles of responsibility and direction assumed by the Bureau of Indian Affairs, then by the Tribal Council, and later by the cattle associations.

Vogt suggests that after long, sustained contact a third "stage" becomes evident, with culture characteristics of the dominant group becoming internalized, not just imitated. This involves a change in the value system of the subordinate culture. The extent and degree of such a change is not easy to determine. At San Carlos it is quite evident that the recent revisions in the structure and operations of the Indian cattle industry indicate some degree of internalization of White values in regard to cattle raising by a portion of the Indians. However, are the majority of the cattle owners merely accepting a new form for their cattle operations, but retaining the old meanings? Agency officials and some of the tribal leaders think that new meanings have also accompanied the new form in the minds of the cattle owners. Only extensive and intensive interviewing of Indian cattlemen, preferably a series of case studies, would provide the real answer to this question.

In his final possible "stage," Vogt suggests that the residuals of Indian value orientations are lost and the Indian culture has ceased to be a reality. Vogt points out that at this "stage" the individual Indian "is culturally indistinguishable from whites of the same age and sex." This writer is doubtful that any individual San Carlos Indian has really reached this final stage, though it is quite possible that some have in regard to values concerning the cattle industry. However, this could be determined best by means of further intensive interviews.

Range steers after roundup on the Victor Livestock Association range.

Registered bulls have greatly improved the quality of the Apaches' cattle.

Part of the IDT herd in a holding pen.

9 CONCLUSIONS

It seems to this writer that the data, and the subsequent analysis of these data, as presented in this report have amply demonstrated the value of certain concepts and principles which have been intended to aid us in understanding the processes involved in directed culture change. Particularly valuable in this respect are Linton's concepts of form and meaning; the principles outlined by Erasmus – empiricism, need, cooperative effort, inducement, and complexity; and Vogt's four "stages" of acculturation.

It was not until agency personnel and tribal officials got together, cooperatively and repeatedly, around the conference table that they became aware of the real needs of the San Carlos cattle industry. Then the complexity of the cattle industry and of its relationships to the rest of the San Carlos Indian culture were realized. Plans were mapped for inducing acceptance of the new program. Empiricism was probably involved only to the extent that the Indian leaders finally realized that they could handle the affairs of the cattle industry and began to do so. A new form was devised for the cattle industry with new meanings attached to it. Then it became the responsibility of the advocates of this change to convince San Carlos cattlemen of the wisdom of the new form and new meanings.

It is the aim of all sciences, social sciences included, to attain positions, based on fact and theory, from which they are able to predict human progress. What is the future of the San Carlos Indian cattle industry? In the technical, mainly non-human, aspects of the San Carlos cattle industry there has been excellent progress. For a good many years cattle raised by San Carlos Indians have consistently classed up with non-Indian cattle. In this respect even greater progress can be confidently expected. It is in the human aspects of the Indian cattle industry that one is on uncertain grounds regarding the future. There are many important variables here that are essentially beyond control. What will the next few years bring in regard to the situations in world, country, state, and local governments? All of these can, and will, have a strong bearing on what happens with the San Carlos Indians. How long will federal services be continued for Indians generally, and more particularly for the San Carlos Indians? When termination of federal control and services comes, what will happen to the reservation area, how will it be handled? What will become of the San Carlos Indians? All of these factors must be considered in any forecast regarding the future of the San Carlos people and their resources.

However, if all these factors remain relatively stable, there should be considerable progress made in the human aspects of the San Carlos cattle industry. The somewhat drastic changes in the cattle program in the last five years have shown the San Carlos cattlemen that they can handle their own affairs. The next five years should see the San Carlos cattlemen making far more efficient use of their reservation resources, and making a real contribution to the San Carlos tribe in return for the use of the reservation resources.

Point of Pines Livestock Association roundup.

Weaned heifers, bawling for their mothers, outside a brushy corral.

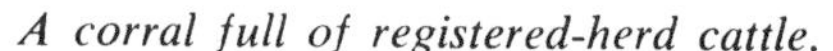

A corral full of registered-herd cattle.

BIBLIOGRAPHY

ANONYMOUS
1948 *San Carlos Hereford Feeder Sales.* San Carlos, Arizona.

BOLTON, HERBERT EUGENE
1936 *Rim of Christendom: A Biography of Eusebio Francisco Kino, Pacific Coast Pioneer.* New York: Macmillan.

BOURKE, JOHN G.
1891 *On the Border with Crook.* New York: Scribner.

CLUM, WOODWORTH
1936 *Apache Agent: The Story of John P. Clum.* Boston: Houghton Mifflin.

CONNELL, CHARLES T.
1921 The Apache, Past and Present. *Tucson Citizen* [Arizona]. Feb. 5–July 31.

ERASMUS, CHARLES J.
1954 An Anthropologist Views Technical Assistance. *The Scientific Monthly,* 78: 147–58.

FISHER, GLEN
1953 *Directed Culture Change in Nayarit, Mexico: Analysis of a Pilot Project in Basic Education.* Middle American Research Institute, Publication No. 17, Part 2 (pp. 65–176). New Orleans: The Tulane University of Louisiana.

GETTY, HARRY T.
1961 San Carlos Apache Cattle Industry. *Human Organization,* 20:4:181–86.

GOODWIN, GRENVILLE
1937 Report on the San Carlos Indian Reservation. MS on file in San Carlos Agency office.
1942 *The Social Organization of the Western Apache.* Chicago: University of Chicago Press.

HODGE, FREDERICK W., GEORGE P. HAMMOND, AND AGAPITO REY
1945 *Fray Alonso de Benivides' Revised Memorial of 1634.* Albuquerque: University of New Mexico Press.

KELLY, WILLIAM H.
1953 *Indians of the Southwest: A Survey of Indian Tribes and Indian Administration in Arizona.* Tucson: University of Arizona, Bureau of Ethnic Research.

LINTON, RALPH
1936 *The Study of Man.* New York: D. Appleton-Century Co.

LINTON, RALPH (ed.)
1940 *Acculturation in Seven American Indian Tribes.* New York: D. Appleton-Century Co.

McCRAY, ERNEST R.
1941 The San Carlos Apache Is a Modern Cattleman. *American Cattle Producer,* 23: 5–8.

RUDO ENSAYO
1951 *Rudo Ensayo, by an Unknown Jesuit Padre, 1763.* Tucson: Arizona Silhouettes. Reprint.

SAUNDERSON, MONT H.
1952 Livestock Production on the San Carlos Apache Indian Reservation: A Study Report. MS on file in San Carlos Agency office.

SLAVENS, THOMAS S.
194– *San Carlos, Arizona, in the Eighties: The Land of the Apache.* Washington, D. C.: Order of Indian Wars.

SPICER, EDWARD H. (ed.)
1952 *Human Problems in Technological Change: A Casebook.* New York: Russell Sage Foundation.
1961 *Perspectives in American Indian Culture Change.* Chicago: University of Chicago Press.

U.S., BUREAU OF INDIAN AFFAIRS
Reports of the Commissioner of Indian Affairs. 1883–86.

U.S., BUREAU OF INDIAN AFFAIRS, SAN CARLOS AGENCY
Annual Reports of the Superintendent. MSS on file in San Carlos Agency office.
1952 San Carlos Withdrawal Report. MS on file in San Carlos Agency office.

U.S., SOIL CONSERVATION SERVICE
1938 Range Surveys Report on the San Carlos Reservation, Arizona. MS on file in San Carlos Agency office.

VOGT, EVON Z.
1951 *Navaho Veterans, A Study of Changing Values.* Papers of the Peabody Museum of American Archaeology and Ethnology, Vol. 35, No. 1. Cambridge, Mass.

. . . .

Files in the San Carlos Agency Office

By-laws for Cattle Associations
Leasing of Land — Permittees
Minutes — Tribal Council
Ordinances
Resolutions
Stock Raising
Stock Raising, Cattle Associations, General
Stock Raising, Cattle Associations, Ash Creek
Stock Raising, Tribal Herd
Tribal Relations

Zeitfracht Medien GmbH
Ferdinand-Jühlke-Straße 7
99095 Erfurt, Deutschland
produktsicherheit@kolibri360.de